THE TEMPLE MOUNT

For the past 4,500 years sacred Mount Moriah in Jerusalem has intrigued people from all over the world. Here, Abraham came to sacrifice his son Isaac, Solomon built the Temple, Jesus taught and Mohammed was transfigured.

In the thirty-six wars which were fought in Jerusalem, this mountain has been the most coveted prize of conquering armies. When destroyed it was rebuilt on ruins. The Temple of Solomon, destroyed by the Chaldeans, was rebuilt by Zerubbabel, only to be destroyed again by Herod the Great. He rebuilt it magnificently and the Wailing Wall still remains.

Today the site is adorned by one of the most beautiful buildings in the world. It covers the slab of limestone rock protruding from its floor, which is believed to have been the one where the altar of the Temple stood.

It is venerated by the followers of the three great religions which grew and were nurtured in Jerusalem: Judaism, Christianity and Islam.

Throughout most of its history the gates of the Temple Mount have been closed to visitors, but today it can be freely visited.

The Temple Mount is both a comprehensive guide and an essential work of reference on this fascinating area of Jewish, Moslem and Christian history.

SOLOMON STECKOLL is an historian and has specialized in Intertestamental Studies with special stress on the Dead Sea Scrolls. Prior to the Six Day War of 1967, he headed excavations at Qumran, in the ancient cemetery, to help beam new light on the Community of the Scrolls and the birth and early development of Christian beliefs.

In 1948, with the birth of the Third Jewish Commonwealth, he took part in the fighting which raged in besieged Jerusalem, during the War of Independence, and has lived in Israel ever since.

Formerly a journalist, Mr Steckoll has travelled frequently in the Arab States, despite living in Israel. After the Six Day War he made a number of trips to Arab capitals, being received by King Hussein of Jordan in Amman and by the late President Nasser in Cairo.

He now divides his time between research, lecturing and writing books. Mr Steckoll is unmarried and lives in Sha'afat an Arab village near Jerusalem.

THE
TEMPLE MOUNT

an illustrated history of
Mount Moriah in Jerusalem

Solomon H. Steckoll

Photography by GARO

Tom Stacey

First published in 1972 by
Tom Stacey Ltd., 28-29 Maiden Lane,
London WC2E 7JP

Copyright © Solomon H. Steckoll 1972

ISBN 0 85468 152 3

Made and Printed in Great Britain by
The Garden City Press Limited,
Letchworth, Hertfordshire SG6 1JS

Author's Dedication

*'And this I hate – not men, nor flag nor race,
but only war with its wild grinning face.'*
(From the *Hymn of Hate* by Joseph Dana Miller.)

I was an eye-witness to two of the thirty-six wars
which raged within Jerusalem and on its holy mountain,
Moriah. The most recent, three days of storm and fury
in the summer of 1967, left over 500 dead in its wake:
soldiers of Israel and Jordan. They died in the fighting
in Jerusalem which ended when the Temple Mount was
taken.
I was a witness in the battlefields to the supreme
valour and courage of the men of both armies
and it is in deep humility that I dedicate this book
to the memory of the fallen of this war, from both camps,
Arabs and Jews.
The focal area in this war was the Temple Mount,
the Baitu-l-Mukaddas, the Habitat of Holiness.
For those who died in this battle,
241 of whom are buried in a communal grave just east
of the city walls of Jerusalem and near Mount Moriah,
one has a conviction that:

*'There shall be
In that rich earth a richer dust concealed.'*

LIST OF ILLUSTRATIONS

To Nebi Samwil
To Ramalla
French Hill
Damascus Gate
Mt of Olives
OLD CITY
Temple Mount
Govt House
Sharafat
ROADS
RAILWAYS
0
1M
To Bethlehem

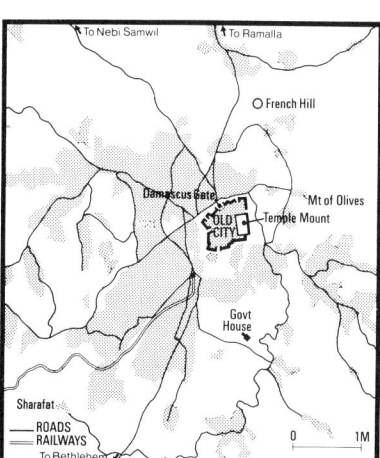

Jerusalem: the modern city

Lions' Gate (St Stephen's Gate)
Antonia
Qaitabay's Fountain
Golden Gate
Dome of the Rock
Dome of the Chain
Kotel Ma'aravi (Western Wall)
El Kas
Moors Gate
El Aqsa Mosque
Robinson's Arch
Solomon's Stables
Southern Wall Excavations
Double Gate
Triple Gate
Single Gate
0
500 FT
Dung Gate

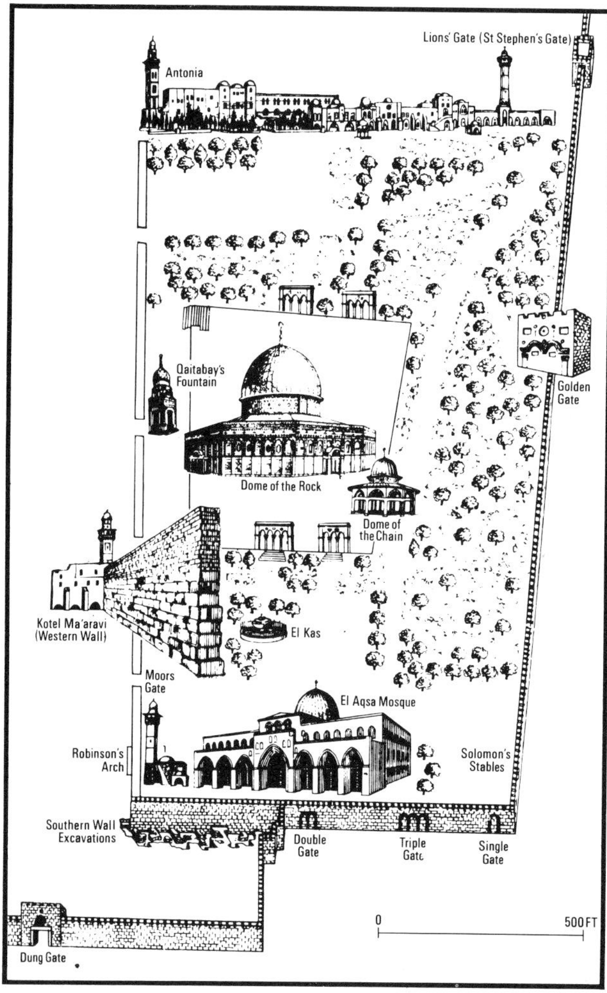

Sketch plan of the Holy Rock

Sketch plan of the Temple Mount

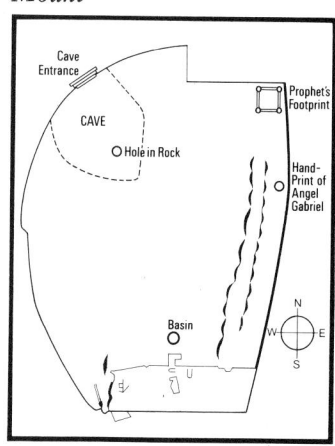

Cave Entrance
CAVE
Hole in Rock
Prophet's Footprint
Hand-Print of Angel Gabriel
Basin
N
W
E
S

There is an outcropping of starkly bare, rough limestone rock in Jerusalem which for thirty centuries past has gripped the minds and hearts of sons of men as being the most sacred spot on earth. Where the Prophet Ezekiel said that Jerusalem was the centre of the world, so this rock on the top of Jerusalem's Mount Moriah is held to be the very heart of the world around which everything revolves and to which everything will return. Numerous myths and legends have developed about this rock where, in fitting tribute to its station, seventy thousand angels guard it at all times, singing paeans of praise to the Most High and remitting the sins of men who come to pray at this spot. It is said that while standing beside this rock one cannot close one's eyelids without them being touched by the wings of numerous angels and that, apart from the permanent guard of the seventy thousand angels whom God changes daily, invisible troops of other angels descend daily to this rock from a direct gate to heaven immediately above it, to sing halleluias.

Man's tribute to the sanctity with which he has endowed this rock, was to build magnificent and beautiful buildings over it. Today there stands the exquisite gold-domed building which many people erroneously call the Mosque of Omar – it is neither a mosque nor was it built by Omar – and in former times the Temple of Solomon stood here, a marvel of beauty of its time.

Traditions, facts and legend blend and mingle here so that it becomes difficult to separate the one from the other. It is held that this was the rock which served as pillow for Jacob and that it was here that Abraham came to undergo the supreme test of his faith to sacrifice his son. Here King David placed the Ark of the Covenant brought by Moses from Mount Sinai, and after his son Solomon built the Temple here, Jews firmly believe that the Unspeakable Name of God is written somewhere on this rock, by the very hand of God Himself. For the Jews there is nothing more holy and awe-inspiring than this secret name of their God, that tetragramaton which must never be pronounced. While the Temple stood, the Ineffable Name of God was pronounced by the High Priest on this sacred spot once a year, on the Day of Atonement. It was held that the immediate destruction of the entire world would ensue should the High Priest, during that fraction of time while speaking the Name of God, have even the slightest impure thought cross his mind.

The rock is no less sacred to Moslems who believe that it was from this sombre hunk of rock that Allah Himself ascended to heaven. When this event occurred, at the beginning of time, Allah turned to this rock and said: 'This is My place and the place of My seat on the Day of Resurrection.' When Allah went up to heaven on completing the creation of all things, Moslem tradition has it, 'the Mighty stretched out His hands towards the places that He wished to point out, saying: "This to the west is the Garden of Eden; this to the east is the fire of hell and this is the place of My scales of justice." '

The Dome of the Rock stands on a platform in an area known to the Jews as the Temple Mount and to Moslems as the Noble Sanctuary. This area with its mosques, domes and arches, all steeped in history and lore, is a walled enclosure at the south-east of the Old City of Jerusalem. The peculiar nature of sanctity of the thirty-four acres in this enclosure, sets it apart not only from other hallowed places in the world, but from the rest of Jerusalem itself. If Jerusalem means anything to the believers in God, then this Mount Moriah is the Jerusalem of their faith. The annals of Jerusalem are of wars and conquests. There is no stone in the city which has not been reddened with human blood in wars and

An old map of Jerusalem

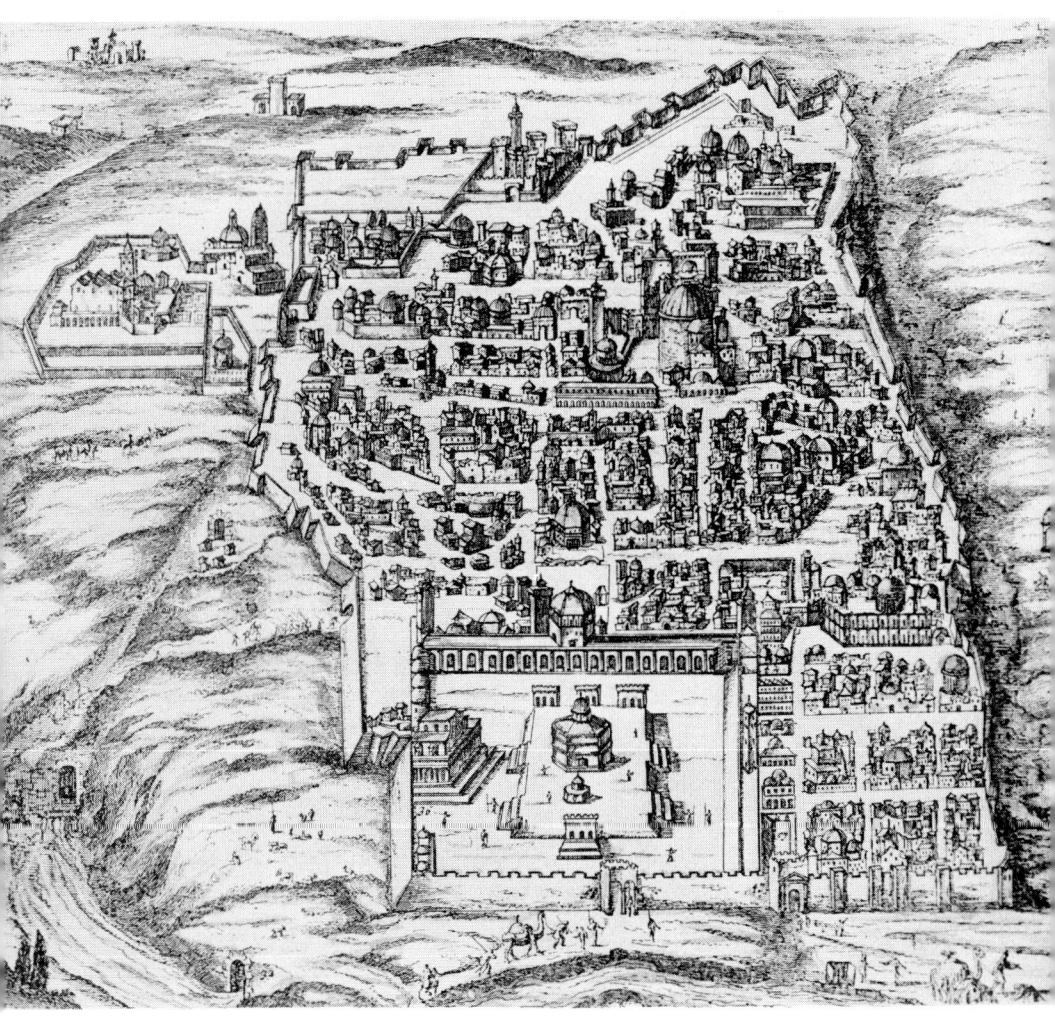

insurrections through the course of the past thirty-five centuries of the recorded history of the city. There is no place where some hand-to-hand fighting has not taken place. The old walls standing and those revealed in archaeological excavations surely echo back the shrieks and cries of despairing and suffering men and women. Through the passage of the ages different nations with various faiths have in turn triumphed in Jerusalem, occupied and built in the city and again suffered defeat at the hands of others – Jews, Pagans, Christians and Mohammedans. The fulcrum of all these battles and blood-lettings, the thoughts which set the spirits of men afire to give them added strength to fight for and win Jerusalem has forever been Mount Moriah and the grey limestone rock at its summit. Few places in the world have been, for the world, as sacred as this city, this flattened mountain top and this rock. While the world lasts and as long as sons of men believe that one spot on it is more sacred and hallowed than another, this will remain so. The deep emotions evoked by the beliefs of sanctity of Moriah have, through the ages – from King David to the present – resulted in many pious acts and much suffering. The bare unadorned rock on Moriah, the cave under it, and many other spots on this holy mount, are tangibles to express what is intangible. Poets have written about these places and a rich lore has grown up to be the adornment of the rock and its surroundings.

I first visited the Temple Mount in January, 1963, at the invitation of the Jordanian Governor of the Old City of Jerusalem, Daud abu Ghazala. The sight which met my eyes as I first saw the extensive plaza dominated by the Dome of the Rock on entering through the Gate of the Chain, was of the tremendous contrast between the closely packed alleys of the Old City through which I had come, and the spaciousness of the Haram-as-Sherif – the

Noble Sanctuary. Then, as I walked on the paved stones, among the plane, cypress and olive trees; looking at the arches on all sides of the platform on which the Dome of the Rock stands in all its glory, the sun glinting on its gold dome, seeing the other domes and fountains, the Aksa mosque; I was overwhelmed by a feeling of peace and tranquillity. Nowhere was this mood stronger than when, having removed my shoes, I entered the Dome of the Rock and, walking on the richly coloured Persian carpets, I looked at the rock pushing up from the marble flags surrounding it. As I stood then, as I did on many subsequent occasions, and looked at this massive rock surrounded by grilles, calm entered me. Calm and a strange feeling on seeing what so many people have never dared to look at; seeing what so many people have died for, looking at and almost being able to touch that rock which, more than any other place, had become a symbol to keep a nation in dispersion and persecution together over a period of thousands of years.

When, in the year A D 333, the Bordeaux Pilgrim came to Jerusalem he found Jews wailing at this rock for the destruction of their Temple and he recorded that they also anointed it with oil. I had come, this first time, from what was simply known as 'the other side', that is from the Israeli sector of Jerusalem, a city divided into two since 1948 without access for the people of either the Israeli or Jordanian sectors, to those of the others. Barbed wire and minefields, concrete walls and soldiers on guard with guns cut the city in two so that my visit to the Old City and especially to the Temple Mount, having been granted permission to enter at the Mandlebaum Gate crossing point, was a unique privilege.

Stormy times have been recorded in the annals of Jerusalem and its Temple Mount. Conquerors came. Fires burnt sacred buildings, igniting even more the spirits of men who witnessed the burning down of their shrines to God. After the death of Joshua, the tribes of Judah and Simeon fought against Jerusalem, 'and took it, and smote it with the edge of the sword, and set the city on fire'. King David took Jerusalem in battle from the Jebusites. The Chaldeans sacked it and destroyed Solomon's Temple. Restored to Judaism by Cyrus, the Temple was rebuilt by Zerubbabel and then, again and again, wars were fought in its precincts. Titus, the Roman, began a siege of Jerusalem in April, the year AD 70 with four Legions; the 5th under Sextus Cerealis, the 10th under Lastius Lepidus, the 12th which had suffered defeat under Cestius and was still in disgrace and the 15th. Titus posted his armies where most conquering forces had encamped prior to doing battle in Jerusalem before him, and since. His 10th Legion was posted on the Mount of Olives, directly east of and overlooking Mount Moriah. The 12th and 15th Legions were posted on Mount Scopus, further to the east and commanding all ways to Jerusalem from the east and north. The 5th Legion was held in reserve. On the 9th August, that historic year, Titus took the city and put it to the torch, burning the Temple which the tyrant Herod had built in place of that of Zerubbabel. Then came Bar Koseba, the Jewish rebel whom Rabbi Akiva called Messiah, only to be crushed by Hadrian who so destroyed Jerusalem at the end of this revolt in AD 135 'as not to leave stone on stone'. Hadrian rebuilt the city as Aelia Capitolina from which Jews were barred. The fate of the Jews was sealed and their dispersion and wanderings and persecutions were sweetened in the time that followed for the eighteen centuries thereafter, by thoughts of the grandeur that was, by thoughts of the Temple which once stood in Jerusalem, on Mount Moriah; and by the hopes and prayers for its restoration. Wars and conquests in

Jerusalem continued apace, for this is the nature of man, and it fell to the Persians when King Chrosroes took it in A D 614 when, in eager anticipation for their redemption, his armies were followed by Jews who flocked to his banner.

On the 14th September, A D 629, the Christians under the Emperor Heraclius took the city. Eight years later Jerusalem fell to Omar who received the capitulation on the Mount of Scopus. Godfrey took it back for the Christians on Friday, the 15th July, 1099. Then a massacre began, the likes of which had not been equalled in the history of the city. Two noted historians, Walter Besant and E. H. Palmer give this description of the horrors in Jerusalem that day. 'The Christians ran through the streets, slaughtering as they went. At first they spared none, neither man, woman nor child, putting all to the sword ... as for the Jews within the city, they had fled to their synagogue, which the Christians set on fire, and so burned them all. The chroniclers relate with savage joy how the streets were encumbered with heads and mangled bodies, and how in the Haram Area, the sacred enclosure of the Temple, the Knights rode in blood up to the knees of their horses. Here more than ten thousand were slaughtered, while the whole number killed amounted, according to various estimates, to forty, seventy, or even a hundred thousand.'

Eighty-eight years later, after a siege which lasted for eight days, while he commanded his armies from Mount Scopus, Saladin pitched his headquarters at the St Stephen's Gate and the Latin Kingdom came to an end. The 2nd October, 1187, Sultan Malek al-Kamil ceded the city to Frederick 11 of Germany during the Fifth Crusade but it was soon recovered for Islam under Hulagu Khan in A D 1244. Jerusalem remained under the rule of the

Sultans of Egypt and Syria until it was conquered by the Turks under Selim 1 in A D 1517 but Britain, France and Russia returned it to the Porte eight years later.

On the 9th December, 1917, the British army conquered Jerusalem and two days later General Allenby entered the city at the Jaffa Gate. At the gate he dismounted and walked into Jerusalem, saying that one cannot enter the holy city of Jerusalem, except in humility, on foot. Fifty years later, the last General to conquer Jerusalem also entered on foot. General Allenby, on entering the walled city of Jerusalem, walked a few paces to the steps of the citadel and read a declaration which expressed in a certain way the emotions which filled him. 'To the inhabitants of Jerusalem, the Blessed,' Allenby began in a voice choked with emotion; 'since your city is regarded with affection by the adherents of the three great religions of mankind, and its soil has been consecrated by the prayers and the pilgrimages of devout people of these three religions for many centuries, therefore do I make known to you ... that all sacred buildings ... will be maintained and protected according to the existing customs and beliefs of those to whose faiths they are sacred.'

Fifty years later, when the Old City of Jerusalem was conquered by the Israeli army under command of General Uzi Narkiss, a similar policy was enforced. It is given to few to be witness when such stirring history is made as to be forever engraved in the annals of Jerusalem. As it was my privilege to walk on the Temple Mount while it was under Jordanian rule, so it was a soul searing experience for me to be on this same compound within an hour of the Israeli conquest on the morning of Wednesday, 7th June, 1967. When, in A D 70, the Roman, Titus, took Jerusalem and burnt the Temple on Mount Moriah, he proclaimed 'Judea Capta', and on that sun-

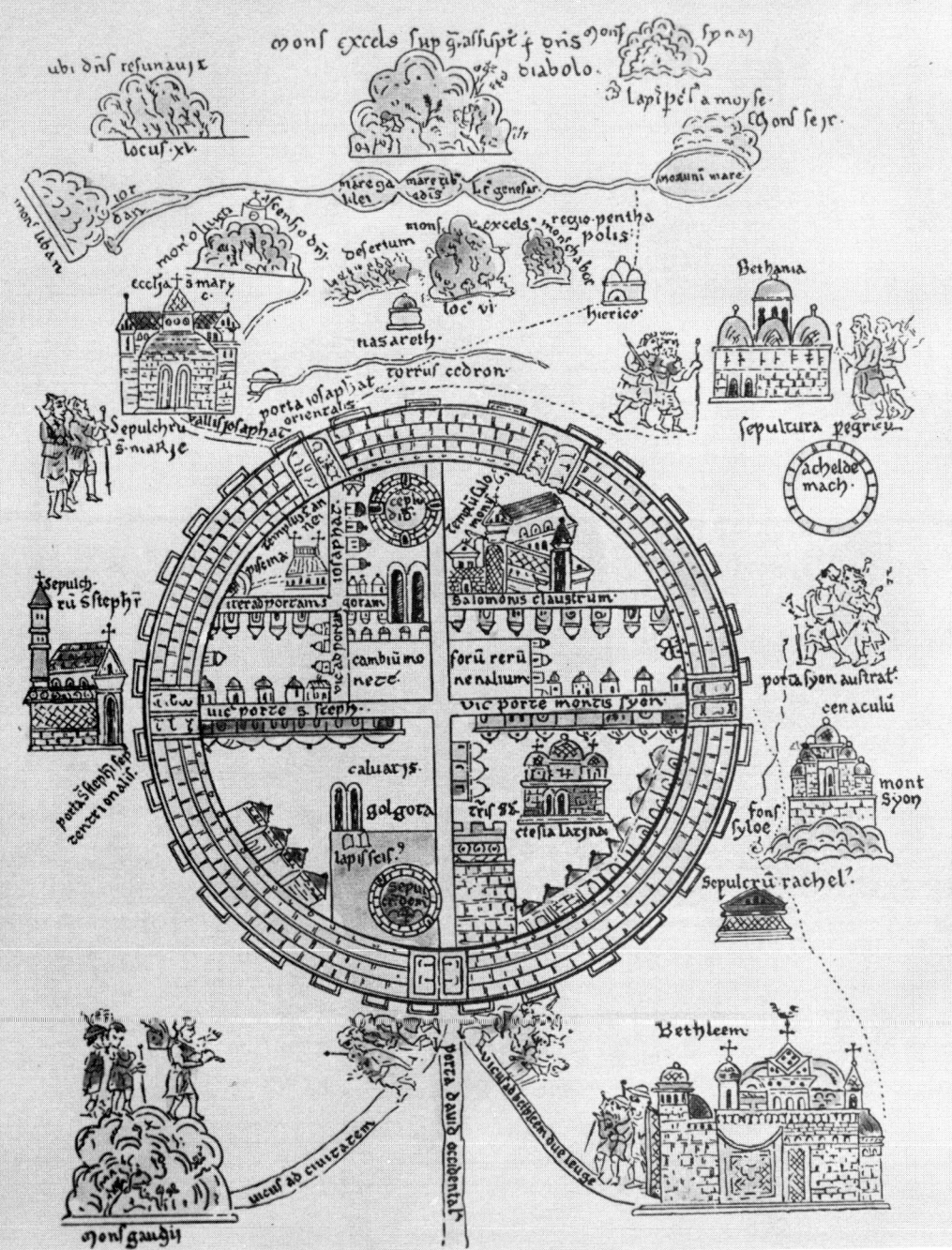

A medieval map of Jerusalem in Latin, intended for the use of Christian pilgrims

soaked morning in June, 1967, when Jewish soldiers stood free and proud on this same Mount Moriah for the first time since that catastrophic day, one could say as I did in an interview that historic Wednesday with a French radio journalist for Radio Europe 1, that 'for the first time since Titus, one can again say, Judea Liberata'.

Moslem tradition has it, that the rock now protected and surrounded by the Dome of the Rock, was the first place from which the waters of the flood receded. On this rock, it is held, the ram's horn will be blown on the Day of Resurrection, and here Allah will gather in His creatures. The Garden of Eden will be transferred to Jerusalem and the Gate of Heaven will open over Jerusalem. On that historic Wednesday, the ram's horn was repeatedly blown, not far off, beside the Wailing Wall where battle-scarred soldiers wept in ecstatic joy to be able to see and touch and kiss the massive Herodian rocks which in more recent times had become a symbol for Jews, giving them a visual, tangible, link to their rich past in this city.

At six o'clock that Wednesday morning, General Narkiss, from his improvised headquarters in Jerusalem gave the orders to Colonel Motta Gur to take the Mount of Olives and move into the walled Old City to capture Jerusalem. Narkiss then drove rapidly to the summit of Mount Scopus from where to direct the battle. He was impatient. Impatient not only to capture Jerusalem but concerned that a United Nations ceasefire could prevent this. Through the din of cannon fire, the screeching screams of supersonic jet fighter planes diving low to attack Jordanian positions, one was still conscious that this was Jerusalem where war was fought, where history was being made. From Scopus, Narkiss looked down on the Temple Mount, the gold dome of the Dome of the Rock reflecting the sun's rays, the silver dome at the southern end of the Aksa mosque, shining in the early morning light. This is Jerusalem. Jewish tradition has it that the celestial Temple is only eighteen miles above the earthly Temple. Moslems believe that this distance is less, only twelve miles.

When General Narkiss gave his orders for the capture of the Mount of Olives and the Old City, surrounded and protected by the solid crenellated stone walls of Suleiman the Magnificent, he did not yet know, as he later told me, of the betrayal of Jordan's King Hussein by the Egyptian General, Abdul Muneim Riad, whom President Abdul Nasser had placed in command of the Jordanian army from 1st June, 1967. In trying to use the Jordanian army only where it could help Egyptian forces who were then fighting a life and death battle with the Israeli army in Sinai, Riad had pulled back most of the troops from Jerusalem and the West Bank, the previous afternoon. The Mount of Olives was quickly taken and from its summit, Colonel Motta Gur now looked directly down into the Temple Mount below him, that Mount Moriah whose loss to Titus, the son of Vespasian, 1,897 years previously, had sounded the death knell of Jewish freedom. Gur gave his orders to the troops to move in to take the Temple Mount as the first stage in taking the Old City. He, too, did not yet know that Riad had evacuated most of the troops. Like his commander Narkiss, like every soldier under his command, Gur was also conscious of the significance of the moment when he ordered his troops to move in. Then Gur could not contain himself to remain high up on the Mount of Olives to overlook the battle and he entered his armoured half track and raced down the hill to the St Stephen's Gate, passing many of the other armoured vehicles which had gone off before. The armoured vehicles smashed through the St Stephen's Gate and swung sharply to the left to enter the Temple Mount at the Gate of the Tribes. It was over. His voice charged with emotion, Colonel Gur switched on his radio to report to Narkiss: 'The Temple Mount is in my hands. Repeat. The Temple Mount is in my hands.' Narkiss replied: 'One hundred per cent. One hundred per cent. I am on my way to you.' Narkiss, accompanied only by his aide Captain Joel and his driver, Sergeant-major Meir, raced down by jeep from Mount Scopus.

The first Israeli army tank to smash through the St Stephen's Gate beside which a bus was burning fiercely, went through at ten to nine that Wednesday morning. After Gur reported to Narkiss, a delegation of Arab religious and lay leaders appeared before the Colonel and surrendered the Old City to him. The jeep of General Narkiss halted outside the St Stephen's Gateway at 09.45. The gate was showing its own wounds caused by the heavy armour which had passed through. From here General Narkiss ran into the Old City, into the Temple Mount and up the steps to the platform of the Dome of the Rock where Colonel Gur was waiting for him. In 1948, during Israel's War of Independence, Narkiss, then a Major, had tried to take the Old City, leading troops into the walled area from the Zion's Gate. Now, nineteen years later, he succeeded in what he failed to do then. Emotions were soaring. History was made. General Narkiss first gave orders to close and guard the doors into the Dome of the Rock and the Aksa mosque to prevent any person from entering. Then he half walked, half ran to the Moor Gate and down a set of twisting steps to the Wailing Wall where battle-scarred soldiers were milling about. Here the Commander stood to attention and sang the Israeli anthem, Hatikva, while one word repeatedly drummed through his mind: 'Shehecheyanu'.

Te Deum laudamus; te Dominum confitemur,
Te aeternum Patrem: omnis terra veneratur.

The guards, placed to protect the building swung open
the heavy brass gate of the western door, of the Dome
of the Rock – the building most sacred to Islam only after
the Kaaba in Mecca – to allow me to inspect whether
it had been damaged in the fighting. Then a single
supersonic jet fighter plane of the Israeli Air force flew
in low from the west, dipping its wings in salute, not
only to the victorious Israeli soldiers below, but to the
Temple Mount and to the rock under the gold dome.

Moslems maintain that this rock fell from heaven about
the time that the spirit of prophesy was imparted. This
holy stone, it is held, wished to accompany the prophet
Muhammed to heaven in his nocturnal flight, but was
restrained by the angel Gabriel in response to the prayers
of Muhammed. The angel Gabriel held the rock so firmly
that the impression of his hand is still pointed out to this
day. It is also believed that the Dome of the Rock contains
God's scales for the weighing of the souls of men, the
shield of the prophet Muhammed, the birds of Solomon,
the pomegranates of King David, the saddle of el-Burak –
Lightning – on which Muhammed made his flight from
Mecca to Jerusalem, as well as the original copy of the
Koran, the parchment leaves of which are four feet long.
For the Jews this is the most hallowed spot on earth, the
threshing floor of Araunah the Jebusite where David
placed the Ark of the Covenant and which later was
believed to have been the site of the Holy of Holies of the
Temple, which glowed beneath the divine manifestation
of the Deity, the Shekinah. Another war had been fought
here but this shrine was undamaged. The doorway of the

Aksa mosque was shot up in the battle and two men died on the Temple Mount that day in June, 1967. Both had been servants of the Haram. One was killed at the southern side of the Dome of the Rock itself and the man's blood stained the veined marble. The second was shot a few yards from the entrance to the underground shelter of the Golden Gate in the eastern wall of the Haram Compound.

That famous Wednesday in June, 1967, was the first day in 780 years, since the occupation of Jerusalem by Saladin, that the muezzin's call for Moslems to come to prayer, was not heard in Jerusalem. The classic phrase, 'bismillah wa-rachman al rachim – in the name of Allah, the Merciful, the Compassionate ...' was not silent for long, however. The three days' fighting in Jerusalem had been fierce and over five hundred people died in the city during this battle, Jews and Arabs. Many thousands were wounded. On the Friday afternoon of the same week a few lonely Moslems prayed in the Haram Court. From the Wailing Wall there came the sounds of the ram's horn – the shofar – still being blown. I stood and watched as these solitary Arabs stood on the paved stones of the large open courts in deep prayer. The sound of prayers of Jews were also heard from the Wall and here, bowing low to the ground as is the custom, prayers to the same One God were softly said.

Yes, love indeed is light from heaven
a spark of that immortal fire
with angels shared, by Allah given
to lift from earth our low desire.

The pillar of Hadrian has been used in the subterranean vaults under El Aksa—through accident or design it appears upside down

(Bottom) An engraving, made according to descriptions in the Bible, of the Temple of Solomon

(Below) This reconstruction of Solomon's Temple was made in 1641

It was on the following Friday, after the thunder of war and the ominous silence which followed in its wake as Jerusalem mourned its dead, that all restrictions were lifted for Moslems to pray on the Temple Mount. By special invitation I was asked to be present inside the Aksa mosque this day, one of the rare, if not the only time in history that a non-Moslem was to be present in the mosque during prayers. At first, from the gloom inside the massive mosque there was but the subdued chanting from the Koran, the only light being that which filtered through the stained glass windows to touch the gold motif of the exquisite gilt decorations on the high ceiling. Then, through the loudspeakers at all corners of the Temple Mount, the words reverberated throughout Jerusalem: 'Hayya 'ala L'fallah, allah akbar, La-Illan-il-Illah' – Come to salvation, Allah is Great, there is no God but God.

I was also to be witness to that terrible fire which burnt in the Aksa mosque two years later, ignited by that self-proclaimed king of Jerusalem, the Australian Michael Rohan, who wanted by this means to hasten the rebuilding of the Jewish Temple, and who was sent to the mad-house after a trial by the Jerusalem District Court.

The name Aksa applies not only to the mosque at the southern side of the Haram Compound, the Noble Sanctuary, but to this entire area. The walled compound is sanctified in every corner. It consists of four stone walls of unequal length and only at the south-west corner is there an angle of the walls of ninety degrees. The south wall is 922 ft long, the east 1,530 ft, the west 1,601 ft and the north wall 1,035 ft long. This is the ground about which a certain Abdallah ibn Salam said to the prophet Muhammed; 'the reason why it is called al-Aksa is because it is in the middle of the world: it is beyond the centre neither on this side nor that'. Upon which the prophet Muhammed replied: 'Thou hast truly spoken.' According to Moslem tradition 'the dawn of the morning and the evening meet in it, which means that the Baitu-l-Mukaddas, the Habitat of Holiness, is in the midst of all wonderful and excellent things'. The hour is fixed by divine decree, Moslems believe, when 'the Masjidu-l-Haram (the mosque at Mecca) shall visit the Baitu-l-Mukaddas (the Jerusalem Haram Compound, the Habitat of Holiness) and they shall both be conducted to Paradise together; and all their inhabitants with them; also the last Judgment and the final reckoning shall be in the Baitu-l-Mukaddas'. Islamic sources say that on the Day of Resurrection the Kaaba of Mecca will be taken to Jerusalem's Noble Sanctuary 'like a bride, together with all the pilgrims who have visited it, and be greeted with the words: "hail to her that visiteth and is visited" '. A tradition delivered by Abdallah ibn Omar has it that 'in heaven, one of the gates to Paradise is always open, whence every morning descend streams of affection and compassion upon the Baitu-l-Mukaddas at a certain moment'. 'Whoever cometh into the Baitu-l-Haram (the mosque of Mecca) shall be forgiven and be advanced eight degrees of beatitude', Moslem belief has it. 'Whoever cometh into the mosque of the Prophet of God (the mosque of Medina) shall be forgiven and be advanced six degrees of beatitude and whosoever cometh into the Baitu-l-Mukaddas shall be forgiven and advanced four degrees.'

It is written that Muhammed was awakened one night by the angel Gabriel in Mecca, who opened his breast and washed the prophet's heart with water from Zamzam. Then a strange beast, el-Burak, was brought and Muhammed rode on its back through the air to Sinai, where God appeared before Moses. He rode on to Bethlehem where Jesus was born and finally to Jerusalem where they alighted on the site of the Temple of Solomon. From the holy rock of Araunah a ladder arose, by which Muhammed ascended to heaven, accompanied by the archangel Gabriel. In the first heaven he met Adam. In the second heaven he saw two rivers, the Nile and the Euphrates and met the prophets Idris and Jesus of Nazareth. In the third heaven he saw the river Kawtar which will be preserved till the end of time. In the fourth heaven he met Aaron and in the sixth heaven the prophet Muhammed met Abraham and Moses. Here the archangel Gabriel waited and Muhammed passed alone into the seventh heaven and found himself in the presence of Allah, from whose lips Muhammed received the series of prayers, now contained in the Koran, to repeat which, even to this day, the muezzin summons the faithful five times a day. It is from this vision on rising from the rock on Mount Moriah that the familiar cry dates, that cry of 'La-Illah-il-Illah ...' There is no God but God. At the beginning of Islam the followers of Muhammed were enjoined to turn to Jerusalem in saying their prayers and only later was the focal point of their faith changed with Jerusalem being replaced by Mecca.

On the south side of this rock the 'footprint' of Muhammed is pointed out, where it was, by tradition and belief, impressed when he ascended to heaven from this spot. The sanctity and awe with which Moslems regard this spot is beyond description and one can but surmise at the shock when, shortly after the Six Day War in 1967, a letter came to the Moslem Council in Jerusalem from a substantial Jewish organization in the United States of America, offering – in all seriousness – to buy the Haram Compound, with the Aksa mosque and the Dome of the Rock with this sacred stone below it, for one hundred million dollars, so that the Jewish Temple could be rebuilt on the site of the House of God of King Solomon.

The Roman Emperor Hadrian, in an effort to leave no trace of the Herodian Temple, destroyed more than a half a century before him by Titus, erected a temple to Jupiter Capitolinus on the site. There was only a single occasion in the long passage of time since then that plans were made to rebuild the Jewish Temple on Moriah. The moving spirit behind this project was the Roman Emperor, Flavius Claudius Julianus, a nephew of Constantine, known as Julian the Apostate because of his opposition to Christianity. He had planned the project in the last year of his reign in AD 363. After annulling all the anti-Jewish laws of his uncle Constantine, Julian issued an edict that the Temple be rebuilt in Jerusalem – an event which gripped the imagination of Jews and led to a frenzy of excitement as Jews from all parts of the known world streamed to Jerusalem to help in the work. Julian supplied the necessary funds and appointed Alypius of Antioch, Governor of Great Britain, to carry out the project. Jews from all over showered from their wealth upon the projected work of rebuilding the Temple and the roads to Jerusalem were clogged by the multitudes of Jewish men and women who, with hopes high, walked up dusty roads. The historians Besant and Palmer recorded that 'hardly were the foundations uncovered, the joyful Jews crowding round the workmen, when flames of fire burst forth from underground, accompanied by loud explosions. The workmen fled in wild affright and the labours were at once suspended. Nor were they ever renewed.' Historians writing of this event, report the belief that the explosion and fire was a manifestation of the anger of God. It is held, however, that the cause for the mysterious flames was not so much a miraculous sign of divine wrath, but the result of noxious gas in the subterranean passages catching fire.

Proposals today, voiced on the whole by Jewish

extremists, to rebuild the Temple which cannot be done without riding rough-shod over Moslem sensibilities and razing the time and custom hallowed shrines of Islam on Moriah, are a cause for bitter conflict in Jerusalem. After the Six Day War the chief chaplain of the Israeli Army, General Shlomo Goren, one of the leading advocates for the rebuilding of the Temple, led demonstrative Jewish prayers in the Haram Compound, causing shock and shivers of apprehension among Moslems as to the fate of their hallowed places of worship.

Great understanding is needed to resolve the conflict which most unfortunately promises to continue with neither side willing nor able to compromise. Conflicts have dogged the history of Mount Moriah which man declared as holy, from the very beginning. Feelings have always run high and emotions sharpened to an edge of hysteria. The present conflict, held more or less under wraps since the Israeli occupation, is no exception to the rough history of Moriah when, in the past, quarter was neither given nor asked in what has been held to be a holy right to defend the compound from 'contamination' by people of other faiths; the whole being confused in associating this with a defence of faith itself. Thus, when the Herodian Temple stood, stone plaques, some in Latin, others in Greek, were placed warning any Gentile not to enter the precincts of the Temple at the risk of losing his life. A number of these signs were found, reading: 'No Gentile is to approach within the balustrade round the Temple and the peribolos. Whosoever is caught will be guilty of his own death which will follow.' While there were no such signs in later times when the enclosure became a sacred place for Islam, Mohammedans were no less jealous to guard the Haram Area from the steps of non-Moslems and threats to kill people trying to enter are

(*Top*) *An accurate reconstruction of Jerusalem as it was in the time of King Solomon*

(*Bottom*) *A 17th-century engraving showing King David and the people of Israel bringing the Ark of the Covenant to Jerusalem*

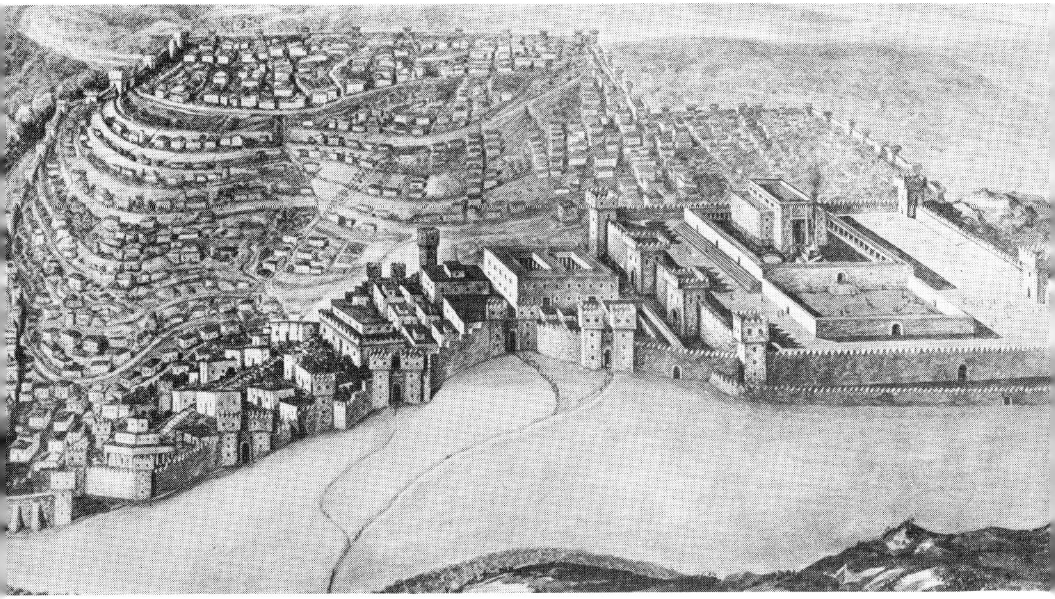

recorded in the reports of travellers who came to Jerusalem in the past. These restrictions were partially lifted in the middle of the nineteenth century but were clamped down again when Arab nationalism rose to a peak under the then Jerusalem Mufti, Haj Amin el Husseini, during the thirties of the twentieth century. In 1948 full Moslem control of the Old City of Jerusalem including the Haram returned to Islamic rule when King Abdullah took that part of the city in the war with Israel. It was his grandson, King Hussein, who was the first person to fully lift restrictions to non-Moslems to visit the Haram Enclosures and the interior of the Dome of the Rock and the Aksa mosque.

Forbidden fruit always attracts and during that time when entry to the Haram Compound was forbidden, many tried to get in, as no doubt they did when the Jewish Temple stood and entry was also forbidden at the risk of death. In the mid-nineteenth century, J. T. Barclay, who finally was allowed to have a quick look inside the Haram Compound, described the conditions relating to the guarding of the sacred area thus: 'So great is the fear inspired by the clubs and cimetars of those blood-thirsty savages, the Mauritanian Africans, to whose jealous custody the entire Haram is committed, that few indeed have been found of sufficient temerity to hazard even the most furtive and cursory reconnoissance of this tabooed spot. It is an ascertained fact [Barclay does not reveal how this 'fact' is ascertained] that every religious community in the Holy City has a firman from the Sublime Porte, empowering them to kill the members of any other communities intruding on their premises; and that the Moslems, at least, delight to execute the decree upon any *infidel*, whether Jew or Christian, that may be caught intruding upon this sacred spot is well known. So wild and ungovernable is their fanaticism that the protection of the Effendis is entirely unavailing ... In 1818 Dr Richardson was officially permitted to make a hasty reconnoissance of it in return for medical services rendered some of the dignitaries of the Haram. And in 1833, Mr Catherwood and his companions, by practicing a bold and hazardous ruze, obtained entrance to nearly every part of the Haram.' Barclay adds the following vignette of that time when the gates to the Haram were firmly barred to those who did not follow the religion of Ibb Islam. 'When the clock of the Mosk needs repairing, they are compelled, however reluctantly to employ a Frank. But in order to have a clean conscience in the commission of such an *abominable piece of sacrilege* as the admission upon the sacred premises, they adopt the following expedient. The mechanic selected being thoroughly purged from his uncleanness by ablution *à la Turc*, a certain formula of prayer and incantation is sung over him at the gate. This being satisfactorily concluded, he is considered as exorcized, not only of Christianity (or Judaism, as the case may be), but of humanity also; and is declared to be no longer a man but a donkey. He is then mounted upon the shoulders of the *faithful*, lest, notwithstanding his depuration, the ground should be polluted by his footsteps; and being carried to the spot where his labours are required, he is set down upon matting within certain prescribed limits; and the operation being performed, he is carried back to the gate, and there, by certain other ceremonies, he is duly *undonkeyfied* and transmuted into a man again.'

The fanaticism of religious Jewry in Israel is no less severe. After the Six Day War, the Wailing Wall was turned into a place of mass worship after bulldozers flattened the houses of Arabs living nearby. A partition was put up to separate men from women at the Wailing Wall, in accordance with the Orthodox Pharisaic Jewish practice. When a group of Jewish leaders of the Reformed congregation in America, who pray – men and women together – wanted to worship at the Wailing Wall in accordance with their practice, this was forbidden them.

For fear of sacrilege of holy places, signs in many languages were placed beside the gates leading to the Haram Compound by the Israeli Rabbinate, forbidding Jews to enter the sacred area. This has not deterred other Jews, among them rabbis, to enter the area and to press for the right of conducting Jewish prayers on Mount Moriah, as a first step to what they call 'full redemption' and the rebuilding of the Jewish Temple. Intolerance is the watchword with little thought of the implications for Jews and Moslems that the Gate of Mercy, part of the double Golden Gate in the eastern wall of the compound is sealed with blocks of hewed stone. While Moriah is the source of strife and contention today, as it was in the past, it remains nevertheless the repository of a rich history and tradition. There are two descriptions on the building of the Temple by King Solomon. The well-known description in the Bible:

And it came to pass in the four hundred and eightieth year after the children of Israel were come out of the land of Egypt, in the fourth year of Solomon's reign over Israel, in the month Zif, which is the second month, that he began to build the house of the Lord. And the house which king Solomon built for the Lord, the length thereof was threescore cubits, and the breadth thereof twenty cubits, and the height thereof thirty cubits ... So he built the house and finished it; and covered the house with beams and boards of cedar ... And the cedar of the house within was carved with knops and open flowers: all was cedar; there was no stone seen ... So Solomon overlaid the house within with pure gold: and he made a partition by the chains of gold before the oracle; and he overlaid it with gold ... And within the oracle he made two cherubims of olive tree, each ten cubits high ... And he set the cherubims within the inner house: and they stretched forth the wings of the cherubims, so that the wing of the one touched the one wall, and the wing of the other cherub touched the other wall ... And he overlaid the cherubims with gold. And he carved all the walls of the house round about with carved figures of cherubims and palm trees and open flowers, within and without. And the floor of the house he overlaid with gold, within and without ...

The Moslem historian al-Siuti gives the following mythical description of how Solomon built the Temple; Solomon the wise who by Jewish and Moslem legend alike was able to converse freely with the animals and birds, understanding their languages, and because of his wisdom and the grace and favour with which God endowed him, was, again according to both Jewish and Moslem tradition, able to converse with the spirits of the netherworld who Solomon used as servants. Says al-Siuti:

When God revealed unto Solomon that he should build him a Temple, Solomon assembled all the wisest men, genii, and Afrites of the earth, and the mightiest of the devils, and appointed one division of them to build, another to cut blocks and columns from the marble mines, and others to dive into the ocean-deeps, and fetch therefrom pearls and coral. Now some of these pearls were like ostrich's or hen's eggs. So he began to build the Temple ... the devils cut quarries of jacinth and emerald. Also the devils made highly-polished cemented blocks of marble ...

The place for the building of the Temple by Solomon was chosen before he began his reign. The Bible relates that:

So the Lord sent a pestilence upon Israel from the morning even to the time appointed: and there died from the people of Dan even to Beersheba seventy thousand men. And when the angel stretched out his hand upon Jerusalem to destroy it, the Lord repented him of the evil, and said to the angel that destroyed the people, It is enough: stay now thine hand. And the angel of the Lord was by the threshingplace of Araunah the Jebusite ... And Gad came that day to David, and said unto him, Go up, rear an altar unto the Lord in the threshingfloor of Araunah the Jebusite ... And David built there an altar unto the Lord, and offered burnt offerings and peace offerings. So the Lord was intreated for the land, and the plague was stayed from Israel.

Tradition and belief has it that this was the same place where David had previously brought the Ark of the Covenant.

So David and all the house of Israel brought up the ark of the Lord with shouting, and with the sound of the trumpet ... And they brought in the ark of the Lord, and set it in its place, in the midst of the tabernacle that David had pitched for it.

The facts as set out in the Bible make it unlikely that the place where the Ark of the Covenant was placed could have been the same spot, that rock, the threshing floor of Araunah the Jebusite, are generally ignored for traditions are strong when religious beliefs are felt and expressed and there is a tendency in such cases not to examine the facts of the matter with too close a scrutiny. Had the tabernacle of Jerusalem where David brought the Ark been the same as the rock where he made sacrifice to intreat God to put an end to the plague, then there would not have been the need for King David first to buy this

An old etching of the Dome of the Rock with the Dome of the Chain in the foreground, and, in the background, a fountain

One of the small cupolas (right) on the Temple Mount with the intricately decorated Dome of the Rock behind it

(Below) An engraving showing the colonnades (right) at the western side of the Temple Mount Compound

threshing floor from Araunah. In religious belief, the rock on Moriah, the Sakhrah under the present Dome of the Rock, is the threshing floor of Araunah where David put his altar and where the Ark had been placed. The belief is equal to religious Jews and Moslems. Islamic historians, in recording the beginning of the building of Solomon's Temple, they say started by his father David, wrote that: 'David, (peace be with him!) saw angels, with flaming swords, ascending by a golden ladder from the Rock into heaven. Then said David: this is the place whereon it is fitting that a Temple should be built to God Almighty. Thus, therefor he built it; but, dying before it was completed, he enjoined Solomon to build it; who built it, and finished it.'

Whether the rock on Moriah was the threshing floor of Araunah three thousand years ago or not, whether this Sakhrah – the sacred rock of Islam – was the exact spot of the Holy of Holies of the Temple, or the spot where the altar stood: are questions which cannot be answered with any degree of accuracy today. The rock is not smooth as a threshing floor should be, but then it is known that the Crusaders chipped off large hunks of this rock to take back to Europe as relics and to sell at high profit. It suffices, perhaps, to know that here, or near this spot, holy buildings stood. Three of the five Temples of the Jews as well as the present Dome of the Rock of Islam.

The considerations which led David and Solomon to build a House of God in Jerusalem were dictated not only by religious impulses but by political considerations, to consolidate Jerusalem as the capital of Israel as against Samaria which had been the centre beforehand. The tribes of Judah and Benjamin, under the kings David and Solomon, gained added control over the people because of this Temple on Moriah. Having built the Temple, Solomon was not deterred from erecting other temples to pagan gods on the same compound, however. 'For Solomon went after Ashtoreth the goddess of the Zidonians, and after Milcom the abomination of the Ammonites. And Solomon did evil in the sight of the Lord, and went not fully after the Lord, as did David his father. Then did Solomon build an high place for Chemosh, the abomination of Moab, in the hill that is before Jerusalem, and for Molech, the abomination of the children of Ammon.' This, no less than the political struggle between the tribes, the struggle for supremacy of Judah and Benjamin with their centre in Jerusalem and of the other ten tribes whose centre was Samaria, led to the split of the kingdom on the death of Solomon. 'What portion have we in David?', the people belonging to the ten tribes then said. 'Neither have we inheritance in the son of Jesse: to your tents O Israel: now see to thine own house, David. So Israel departed unto their tents.' The kingdom was split and a Temple was built on Mount Gerizim in Samaria, which never, however, succeeded in gaining that general support of the people as the Jerusalem Temple. Or, perhaps, this conclusion could be drawn only because the history of those times is that which was mostly recorded by followers of Judah and Jerusalem.

And it came to pass in the ninth year of his reign, in the tenth month, in the tenth day of the month, that Nebuchadnezzar king of Babylon came, he, and all his host, against Jerusalem, and pitched against it ... And on the ninth day of the fourth month the famine prevailed in the city, and there was no bread for the people of the land ... And the city was broken up ... And in the fifth month, on the seventh day of the month, which is the nineteenth year of king Nebuchadnezzar king of Babylon, came Nebuzaradin, captain of the guard, a servant of the king of Babylon, unto Jerusalem. And he burnt the house of the Lord.

This cataclysmic event occurred in the year 586 B C. Half a century later the first exiles from Babylon returned to Jerusalem with Zerubbabel and a beginning was made to rebuild the Temple, work which was completed seventy years after its destruction. 'And this house was finished on the third day of the month Adar, which was the sixth year of the reign of Darius the king.'

The Ark of the Covenant which had been in the Holy of Holies of Solomon's Temple, was lost without any trace to this day after the Chaldeans sacked Jerusalem. Only Solomon's Temple could boast of the Ark, the Mercy Seat, the Shekinah, the Holy Fire and the Urim and Thummin. But the Temple of Zerubbabel became the fount of Jewish piety and the fulcrum around which Jewish national and religious thoughts turned. The Second book of Maccabees relates that 'when the holy city was inhabited in unbroken peace, and the laws were kept right strictly ... it came to pass that even kings themselves did honour the Place and glorify the temple with the noblest presents'.

Now began the first of a series of events which, with political ambitions and designs given precedence by many notables in Jerusalem, led to stark tragedy and the eventual collapse of Jewish independence. It is recorded that in the year 174 or 175 B C., a certain notable, a Benjamite, Simon, the warden of the Temple, 'fell out with the high priest' and unable to get the better of the high priest, Onias, Simon 'betook himself to Apollonius of Tarsus, then governor of Caelesyria and Phoenicia, and informed him that the treasury in Jerusalem was full of such untold sums of money that the wealth of the funds was past counting'. Apollonius told the king, Seleucus I V, who sent his chancellor, Heliodorus, to Jerusalem with orders to take these funds from the Temple, since Simon had said that these moneys did not rightly belong to the Temple and was not to be considered 'sacred funds'. Heliodorus went to the high priest in Jerusalem and demanded the money. Onias replied that 'in all there were four hundred talents of silver and two hundred of gold; it was utterly impossible, he added, that injury should be inflicted on those who had put their trust in the sacredness of the Place and in the majesty and inviolable sanctity of the Temple, honoured all over the world'. When Heliodorus entered the Temple to confiscate the funds he was, however, confronted by angels who scourged him out of it more dead than alive. The second Book of Maccabees describes the scene thus: 'Heliodorus proceeded to execute his orders. But when he and his guards had got as far as the front of the treasury, the Sovereign of spirits and of all authority prepared a great apparition, so that all who had presumed to enter were stricken with dismay at the power of God and fainted with sheer terror. For there appeared to them a horse with a terrible rider, and it was decked in magnificent trappings, and rushing fiercely forward it struck at Heliodorus with its forefeet. And the rider seemed to be armed with a golden panoply. Two youths also appeared before Heliodorus, remarkable for their strength, gloriously handsome, and splendidly arrayed, who stood by him on either side, and scourged him unceasingly, inflicting on him many sore stripes.'

Intrigues continued among the priests in Jerusalem and, on the death of Seleucus and the beginning of the reign of his son Antiochus who called himself Epiphanes (the great) and whom the Jews were to call Epimanes (the madman), gave added power to the evil priests in Jerusalem who succeeded in driving out the legitimate high priest and taking control. An event was now to occur which, more than any other, was to leave its indelible mark not only on the history of Jerusalem and its Temple, but indeed on the history of mankind. The internal power struggle in Jerusalem led one faction to call for the help of Antiochus, who, when he took Jerusalem in 170 BC, put a halt to the Temple sacrifice and began a ruthless policy to suppress the Jewish religion and enforce Hellenism. The anguish of the Jews was at once real and quivering and to endure in the faith during the persecutions of Antiochus Epiphanes became a supreme effort of the human soul. The viciousness and violence of the persecution of the Jews at that time was extreme. The tenacity of the Jews in the face of the horrors was staunch. Antiochus began his reign of terror to try and enforce the 'final solution' and wipe the Jewish religion off the face of the earth, with the capture of Jerusalem – an event and that which followed, described in contemporary records as follows: 'He therefore started from Egypt in a fury, stormed the city, and commanded his soldiers to cut down without mercy any one they met, and to slay those who sheltered in their houses. So there was a massacre of young and old, and extermination of boys, women and children, a slaughter of virgins and infants. In the short space of eight days eighty thousand were destroyed ... not content with this, he dared to enter the most holy temple on earth, under guidance of Menelaus, who proved himself a traitor both to the laws and to his country.'

This marked both the beginning of the revolt led by the five sons of Hashmon, the most commanding personality of whom was Judas Maccabeus; and the rise of apocalyptic thought and literature which was to inspire and influence many in a later age: the Teacher of Righteousness of the Community of the Dead Sea Scrolls, John the Baptist and Jesus of Nazareth. The most influential prophet to inspire those who followed with the concept of the apocalypse was Daniel. He recorded that the conquest of Jerusalem and desecration

The Dome of the Rock or mosque of Omar is one of the finest examples of Islamic architecture. Built between 669 and 692 AD it has a magnificent gilded cupola and coloured decorative motifs on its walls

Exterior view of the Dome of the Rock showing the 'scales of justice' and the steps leading up to them on the right

*Interior of the Dome of the Rock, with decorated colonnades and in the centre, the
Holy Rock*

*(Previous spread) Aerial view of the Temple Mount, showing the octagonal Dome of the
Rock in the centre with the Aksa mosque behind it*

The interior of the Dome of the Rock showing the Holy Rock.
A number of recesses both on its surface and below have been
cut into it and are said to indicate the spots at which
Abraham, Elijah, David and Solomon prayed

of the holy Temple by Antiochus until its restoration by
the Hasmoneans; as he put it: 'from the time that the
daily sacrifice shall be taken away, and the abomination
that maketh desolate set up, there shall be a thousand two
hundred and ninety days'. This time of three and a half
years roughly corresponds with other records which say
that the Temple was re-consecrated three years and two
months after it was made a heathen altar by Antiochus.

In the year 161 BC, Judas the Maccabee deposed the
high priest Alcimus who went to King Demetrius to ask
for help in restoring him to his post in the Jerusalem
Temple. It is written that Demetrius then summoned
Nicanor, 'formerly master of the elephants, and appoint-
ing him governor of Judaea, he dispatched him with
written instructions to make away with Judas and to
scatter his troops and to set up Alcimus as high priest of
the great temple'. What happened then is a story which
has been told and re-told in the generations which followed. After first making friends with Judas in Jerusalem,
Nicanor, ordered by his king to take the man captive,
went 'to the great and holy temple, while the priests were
offering the usual sacrifices, and commanded them to
deliver up the man. And when they swore they did not
know where the man was whom he sought, he stretched
forth his right hand toward the sanctuary, and swore this
oath: Unless you hand over Judas as my prisoner, I will
raze this shrine of God to the ground, and break down the
altar, and erect on this spot a temple of Dionysus for all
to see.'

A fierce battle was fought between Judas and Nicanor
in Samaria which ended in the victory of the Jews. It is
written that when, after the battle, 'they recognized
Nicanor lying dead in full armour; a shout of excitement
arose, they blessed the Sovereign Lord in the language of
their fathers'. Judas then 'ordered Nicanor's head and

arm to be cut off and carried to Jerusalem. When he arrived there, and had called his countrymen together and set the priests before the altar, he sent for the garrison of the citadel, showed them the vile Nicanor's head and the impious creature's hand which he had stretched out vauntingly against the holy house of the Almighty ...'

When Antiochus Epiphanes held Jerusalem, suppressing the Jewish religion and establishing a gymnasium in the city, so indispensable for the furtherance of Greek culture, he was by no means opposed by all the Jews. While the Maccabaeans and other defenders of the faith rose in revolt, many among the younger members of the Jewish aristocracy in Jerusalem eagerly formed a body of *epheboi*, and flaunted about in the streets in those clothes which corresponded to the Greek country dress, the ephebic chlamys and broad-brimmed hats.

It was, however, the self proclaimed defenders of the faith who, after restoring Jewish worship in the Temple on Mount Moriah, themselves violated the rules regulating the office of the high priest of the Temple and in their unquenchable thirst for power, the Hasmonean rulers usurped, for themselves, the function of the high priests. The last rightful holder of this position, decreed to be of the family of Zadok since the first Temple of Solomon, fled to Egypt and erected a Temple at Leontopolis in 154 BC. In Jerusalem, sacrifices were still made on the altar beside Zerubbabel's Temple on Moriah, while strife and contention continued unbated as the Temple was utilized by successive rulers more and more as a means to further their power and influence rather than for purely religious purposes This blending of politics with religion, the exploitation of man's belief in God, at that time, finds its echoes in our time where the same attitudes are evoked regarding this same Mount Moriah and the control over it

The exploitation of the sacred Temple and its precincts for political purposes, rather than restricting it to the worship of God by the Jews during the Hasmonean and Herodian periods, as in present time following the Israeli conquest in 1967; is by no means confined to the Jews. The Moslems, particularly during the twentieth century, have also so exploited the hallowed Compound of the Haram. The leader of the Arab revolt during the First World War; Hussein ibn Ali, Sherif of Mecca and great grandfather of the present head of the Hashemite dynasty, King Hussein of Jordan, was buried in a room in the western cloisters of the Haram Compound on his death in 1931. This was when the Arab nationalistic struggle in Palestine was at a peak and it was felt by Islamic leaders that the tomb of Hussein ibn Ali in the holy ground would act as a rallying point in their revolt. The then Mufti of Jerusalem, Haj Amin el Husseini, to gain the support of the Moslems of the Indian sub-continent in this political struggle, ordered that an Indian Moslem leader, Muhammed al-Hindi, be also buried in these cloisters. A signal honour which did not, however, achieve the expected results at that time. During the 1948 war in the Holy Land following the United Nations decision on the establishment of independent Jewish and Arab States in the country, one of the Arab leaders in the fighting against the Jews, Abdul Kader el-Husseini, was killed in a battle on the hilltop village of Kastel near Jerusalem and Abdul Kader became the third person to be buried in the cloisters of the Haram – again for political reasons.

The connection with and devotion to Jerusalem having been decreed by the prophet Muhammed in the second sura of the Koran, his followers set their hearts and swords to capture the city from the Christians so that they could worship at the Baitu-l-Mukaddas, the Habitat of Holiness, as decreed by the prophet. The head of the army of Islam was Abu 'Obeidah ibn el Jerrah. The followers of the prophet Muhammed rode in battle array into the Holy Land. The Byzantine Emperor Heraclius was defeated at Yarmuk and Abu 'Obeidah prepared to march on Jerusalem. A detachment of five thousand men was sent in the van under Yezid ibn Abi Sufiyan while Abu 'Obeidah followed with the main body of his troops going out in the first jehad – holy war – of Islamic history. The Commander of the Islamic forces was joined at the approaches to Jerusalem by another division under 'Amer ibn el 'As. Jerusalem fell without a battle, although there were protracted negotiations for its surrender. Abu 'Obeidah first sent a demand for capitulation of the city calling on the Christians either to embrace Islam or pay a tribute of unbelievers. 'If you refuse,' he warned, 'you will have to contend with people who love the taste of death more than you love wine and swine's flesh. You may rest assured that I will come up against you, and will not depart until I have slain all the able-bodied men among you, and carried off your women and children captive.' The Christians in beleaguered Jerusalem agreed to capitulate but insisted that they surrender only to the Caliph Omar himself. A messenger was sent post haste to Medina to summon Omar who, according to historians, came up to Jerusalem dressed in such simplicity and with so modest a bearing, that the Christian Patriarch of Jerusalem would not at first believe that this was the great leader of all Islam. 'Omar was mounted on a camel and attired in simple Badawi costume, a sheepskin cloak and coarse cotton shirt; Abu 'Obeidah was mounted on a small she-camel, an "abba" or mantle of haircloth, folded over his saddle, and a rude halter of twisted hair forming her only trappings. He wore his armour and carried his bow slung across his shoulders.

Abu 'Obeidah, dismounting from his beast, approached the Caliph in a respectful attitude, but the latter, dismounting almost at the same moment, stooped to kiss his General's feet.' Omar then entered the Moslem camp on the Mount of Olives and it was here that the Patriarch, Sophronius, came to surrender Jerusalem to him.

While looking down at Jerusalem from the height of the Mount of Olives, Omar sent for and spoke at length with a Jerusalem Jew who had converted to Islam during the lifetime of the prophet Muhammed. Omar asked this man, a certain Ka'ab by name, to tell where the Jewish Temple had stood, for this was the place where the Prophet of Arabia had ascended to heaven and was thus the true Baitu-l-Mukaddas – the Habitat of Holiness – where the followers of Muhammed were to pray. 'Where was the temple of David and Solomon, abu Ishak,' Omar asked Ka'ab, who pointed far below saying that the holy place was where the Christians had thrown a heap of dung on a rock. The site of the Temple had, indeed, been systematically defiled by the Christians of that time out of abhorrence for the Jews. Eutychius wrote that 'when Helena, the mother of Constantine, had built churches at Jerusalem, the site of the rock and its neighbourhood had been laid waste and so left. But the Christians heaped dirt on the rock so that there was a large dung hill over it.' On receiving the capitulation, the first move of Omar was to ask the Patriarch Sophronius to lead him to the site of the Temple, or as Moslem historians state, 'the place of adoration of David'. The Caliph did not, however, tell the Patriarch that he had already received information from Ka'ab as to where the holy ground was to be found. Sophronius led Omar, accompanied by four thousand of his attendants into the city, and first took him to the Church of the Holy Sepulchre, saying that this was the site of Solomon's Temple. 'Thou liest,' Omar replied

Interior view of the Dome of the Rock's cupola

curtly, whereupon the Patriarch led him to Mount Zion and here maintained firmly that this was the site of the Temple. Again Omar told him that he was lying, whereupon the Patriarch led the procession to the Temple Mount and halted at the gate called Muhammed. Contemporary historians relate that 'the dung had settled on the steps of the gate in such quantities that it came out into the street in which the door was situated, and nearly clung to the roofed archway of the street. Hereupon the Patriarch said, "We shall never be able to enter unless we crawl upon our hands and knees." ' Omar replied that, in that case, 'on our hands and knees be it', and motioned the Patriarch to precede him, and so they entered the Compound.

After standing in silence for some time Omar suddenly announced that: 'By Him in whose hands my soul is, this is the place of David, from which the Prophet told us that he ascended into heaven.' The Caliph Omar then began moving the dung off the rock with his sleeve, whereupon his attendants immediately followed in like manner until it was cleaned and only now could the Saracens look at the rock itself which was destined to become so important to their faith. About this rock, it is written, that God, 'on the day of judgment, will change the Sakhrah into white coral, enlarging it to extend over heaven and earth. Then shall men go from that Rock to heaven or hell, according to that great word, "there shall be a time when this earth shall change into another earth, and the heaven shall turn white; the soil shall be of silver; no pollution shall ever dwell thereon". In the law, God says to the Rock of the Holy Abode, Thou art my seat; thou art near to me: from thou foundation have I raised up the heavens, and from beneath thee have I stretched forth the earth ... Who dies within thee, is as if he died within the world of heaven, and who died around thee, is as if he died within thee.'

With such belief in the sanctity of this rock, it soon became a tenet of faith that all the great prophets, since the creation of the earth, had come to pray on this rock. There are a number of recesses cut into the rock, both on its surface and below it, the latter to be seen from the cave under the Sakhrah, indicating the spots where Abraham, Elijah, David and Solomon had prayed. The nineteenth-century explorer and historian, J. T. Barclay, writes about the Sakhrah that 'it is a well known fact among men that this rock is suspended between heaven and earth. It is said that it remained so suspended until a pregnant woman, when she had entered under the rock, being terrified with this appearance, miscarried there. Then it was surrounded with the present building, to conceal the terrific marvels of the place.'

This is no doubt based on Islamic lore about the rock and the cave below it, that cave which during the Latin Kingdom of Jerusalem was called the 'Confessio', held by the Crusaders to have been the place where Jesus met the woman taken in adultery. The cave, entered by going down a set of steep steps at the southern side of the rock, is some eight feet high, while its ceiling is some four or five feet below the upper surface of the rock. This Noble Cave is considered to be, perhaps, the most sacred spot of all to be found on earth. There is a hole piercing it to the top of the Sakhrah, while, in stamping on the floor of the cave one hears hollow sounds so that, undoubtedly, there are further subterranean chambers or passages below the cave itself. When the northern wall of the cave is struck, hollow sounds are also clearly heard so that it is clear that the support here for the massive rock above is nothing more than a partition and that there is a vacant area beyond. To knock so on the glass protected walls or stamp on the floor of the cave today will bring forth the wrath of the guardians of the Dome of the Rock and such a venture could be undertaken, if not at the risk of one's life, certainly at the risk of one's limbs, quite apart from inflaming Moslem sensibilities in their holy place. The 'well known fact' of Barclay that the Sakhrah at one time stood suspended in the air, is probably based on the account of a certain Messir-el-Ghoram who recorded that 'when I would enter there [under the rock] I feared that it would sink down under the burden of my sins. But, having seen that sinners covered with all kinds of iniquity entered and came out safe and sound, I took courage to enter. I still hesitated, however. At last I entered, and was astounded to see the rock detached on all sides, and not joined to the earth.'

In the year A D 684, the ninth successor of Muhammed and fifth Caliph of the House of Omawiya, 'Abd al-Melik decided to build a dome over the rock and a mosque in the Temple Enclosure in Jerusalem. This was dictated not only by the sacredness of the area and the injunction of the prophet Muhammed himself that the faithful must turn to pray to this spot, but by political considerations as well. The inhabitants of Mecca and Medina had risen in revolt against the legitimate Caliph and had appointed a certain Abdallah ibn Zobeir as their spiritual and temporal leader. To regain full support of Mohammedans and to detract, in part, from the central function of pilgrimage of Mecca and Medina, 'Abd al-Melik decided to turn Jerusalem into a major centre for Islam as it had been at the beginning, during the lifetime of the prophet Muhammed. The Caliph sent the following proclamation to all his dominions. ''Abd al-Melik, desiring to build a dome over the Holy Rock of Jerusalem, in order to shelter the Moslems from the inclemency of the weather, and, moreover, wishing to restore the mosque, requests his subjects to acquaint him with their wishes on the matter, as he would be sorry to undertake so important a matter without consulting their opinion.' This turned out to have been an astute approach and support came from all parts of the Moslem world. Al-Melik fixed as a budget for building the Dome of the Rock, a sum equivalent to the entire revenue of Egypt for seven years. He appointed two men to be in charge of the building of both the Dome of the Rock and the Aksa mosque, Rija ibn Haiyah al-Kendi and Yezid ibn Sallam; whose first task was to erect a building to house the vast treasures from which they would draw through the years in completing these two massive and magnificently beautiful buildings. This treasury stands directly to the east of the Dome of the Rock, a most interesting building today known as the Dome of the Chain, the Cubbet as-Silsela. On completing the building of the Dome of the Rock in AD 691, Rija and Yezid found there were still some funds left over and they so informed the Caliph. 'Abd al-Melik ibn Marwan told them to accept this sum, of a hundred thousand dinars, in payment for their work. They refused to accept this, however, and used the money to plate the dome with gold. Rija and Yezid also surrounded the Sakhrah inside the building with a latticed screen of ebony and hung brocaded curtains above the holy rock between the pillars. Tradition has it that, in the time of 'Abd al-Melik, a precious pearl, the horn of the ram sacrificed by Abraham in place of his son and the crown of Chosroes were attached to a chain which is suspended from the centre of the dome but that, when the Caliphate passed into the hands of the Beni Hashem, the latter removed these relics to the Kaaba in Mecca.

The Cubbet as-Sakhrah, the Dome of the Rock, is a building of symmetry, grace and beauty. The lower part of the building is a true octagon, with each side measuring sixty-seven feet so that the diameter of the building is some 170 ft. This is also the height of the building, the central and elevated portion of which is circular. It is generally believed that the Dome of the Chain was first built as a smaller model for the Dome of the Rock but this is not so, since the Dome of the Chain is a decagon and not an octagon as the central building which today graces the Haram as-Sherif. It is recorded that the design of the Dome of the Rock, later decorated with the multi-coloured Persian tiles of rich blues, yellows and greens, was planned to symbolize the centre of the world in its inner circle of pillars and that the two octagons inside represent the mainland and the ocean. This interpretation follows Islamic conceptions similar to those of the Jewish sages, such as that given by Abba Yose b. Hannan, in the name of Semuel ha-Kattan:

This world resembles the ball of the human eye. The white of the eye is the ocean, which encompasses the whole world, the black of the eye is the inhabited world, the pupil of the eye is Jerusalem, and the human face reflected in it is the Temple (may it soon be rebuilt, in our days and in the days of all Israel).

There is an inscription, in mosaic, in outstanding ornate Cufic script, running round the colonnade of the dome. The name of the builder of the building, 'Abd al-Melik, was erased at a later date and the name of Abdullah al-Mamun put in its place. The forgers who wished to honour al-Mamun in this manner, and his name is there to this day, to be seen by those who can decipher the writing, did not erase or change the original date in the inscription however, and from this it is known that the original dedication was indeed to 'Abd al-Melik. This inscription expresses a great deal about the piety which accompanied the erection of this building, the sanctity with which it was held and its place of hallowness in

Interior of the Dome of the Rock showing the Rock itself and the colonnades surrounding it

(Below) A literal translation of this 1st century A.D. Greek inscription reads: 'No Gentile is to approach within the balustrade round the Temple and the peribolos. Whosoever is caught will be guilty of his own death which will follow.'

Islam today. Since it is extremely difficult to come by a complete rendering of this inscription, it is given here, in translation, in full. It reads:

In the name of Allah, the Merciful, the Compassionate. There is no God but God. He has no partner. His is the kingdom, His the praise. He grants life and death, for He is the Almighty. In the name of Allah, the Merciful, the Compassionate. There is no God but God. He has no partner. Muhammed is the prophet of God, pray God for him. The servant of God, Abdallah, the Imam of Mamum [this name subsequently inserted instead of the original name of 'Abd al-Melik ibn Marwan], Commander of the Faithful, built this dome in the year 72 [AD 691]. May God accept it at his hand, and be content with him, amen. The building is complete, and to God be all praise. In the name of Allah, the Merciful, the Compassionate, there is no God but God. He has no partner. Say, He is the One God, the Eternal. He neither begetteth nor is begotten and there is none like Him. Muhammed is the prophet of God, pray God for him. In the name of Allah the Merciful, the Compassionate. There is no God but God, and Muhammed is the prophet of God, pray God for him. Verily, God and His angels pray for the prophet. O, ye who believe, pray for him and salute him with salutations of peace. In the name of Allah, the Merciful, the Compassionate. There is no God but God, to Him be praise. He taketh not unto Himself a son, and none can be a partner to His kingdom and no lower creature can be His associate. Magnify ye Him. Muhammed is the prophet of God; God Himself, His angels and prophets pray for him, peace be upon him and the Mercy of God. In the name of Allah, the Merciful, the Compassionate. There is no God but God. He has no partner. His is the kingdom and His all praise. He grants life and death, for He is Almighty. Verily, God and His angels pray for the prophet. O ye who believe, pray for

him, salute him with salutations of peace. O ye who have
received the Koran, exceed not the bounds of your religion
and speak naught but truth about God. Verily, Jesus the
son of Mary is the prophet of God. God cast His word over
Mary and a spirit from Him. Believe then in God and His
prophets and do not say that there are three gods; forbear
and it will be better for you. God is but One. Far be it from
Him that he should have a son. To Him belongeth what-
soever is in the heaven and in the earth and God is a
sufficient protector. Jesus does not disdain to be a servant of
God, nor do the angels who are near the throne. Whosoever,
then, disdains His service and is puffed up with pride, God
shall gather them all at the last day. O God, pray for Thy
prophet Jesus, the son of Mary. Peace be upon me the day I
am born and the day I die, and the day I am raised to life
again. So too for Jesus, the son of Mary, concerning whom
ye doubt. It is not for God to take unto Himself a son, far be
it from Him. If He decree a thing, he does but say unto it:
Be, and it is. God is my Lord and yours. Serve Him for this
is the right way. God has testified that there is no God but
He; and the angels and spirits endowed with knowledge
testify it and that He executes righteousness. There is no God
but He, the Mighty, the Wise. Verily, the true religion in the
sight of God is Islam. Say praise be to God who taketh not
unto Himself a son, as none can be a partner to Him in the
Kingdom. No lower creature can be His assistant. Magnify
ye Him.

There can be but little doubt that, had the Crusaders
managed to read this inscription which repeatedly con-
tradicts basic beliefs of Christians, that it would have
been effaced. When the Crusaders did take Jerusalem,
they turned the Dome of the Rock into a church, as they
did with the al-Aksa mosque. In 1060 the great can-
delabra suspended from the dome in the Cubbet

55

as-Sakhrah, containing five hundred candles, suddenly collapsed and fell with a terrible crash on to the holy rock itself. This accident was looked on with forboding by Moslems who saw it as a sign of a great calamity to Islam. These fears were not unfounded since the Crusader conquest of Jerusalem followed soon afterwards. The Franks built an altar on the Sakhrah after covering it with white marble and here they placed a large cross, plated with gold and studded with jewels. These were removed by Saladin when he retook Jerusalem. Saladin also ordered that the frescoes which the Crusaders had painted on the walls of the Dome of the Rock, be covered up. Remains of these frescoes, representing Jacob's Vision at Bethel, and the Presentation in the Temple with Latin verses inscribed beneath and around them, were still visible when the marble facing which Saladin had ordered erected, was partly removed in 1873.

Many earthquakes struck Jerusalem in its history, some of them causing considerable damage to the Dome of the Rock and to the Aksa mosque. It is recorded, however, that when a fearful earthquake convulsed the Holy Land in AD 1068, that the Sakhrah, the holy rock, was rent asunder by the shock and the cleft then miraculously reclosed.

If Abdallah, the Imam of Mamun, and son of Haroun el Rashid had his name placed without right in the inscription of mosaic in the Dome of the Rock, it could at least be said of him that he completed the building of the great Aksa mosque in AD 831, the building of which was begun by al-Melik in AD 709. There is room for more than five thousand people to pray inside the Aksa which, apart from its more modern additions on its eastern wing is 280 ft long and 183 ft wide. In AD 1118 the Aksa mosque was assigned to the Knights Templars headed by Hugh de Payens and Geoffrey de St Aldemar who used the vast underground chambers now known as Solomon's stables, to stable their horses, and the mosque itself as a church. At that time it was called the Palace of Solomon while the Dome of the Rock was called the Temple of Solomon. According to some historians, the murderers of Thomas à Becket were buried in front of the Aksa. There is no way of determining whether this is true or not but it was at the entrance to the Aksa mosque that a king was slain in our times. It was on Friday, the 13th June, 1951, immediately before prayers in the Aksa mosque that King Abdullah was shot dead by an assassin as he arrived to pray. A bullet, deflected by a medal on his uniform, also came close to killing the stricken monarch's grandson who was with him, a youth of sixteen who was destined to become the present King Hussein of Jordan. It was after Hussein became king that he ordered the restoration of the shrines on the Haram Compound, including the new coating of gold and aluminium alloy which today graces and enhances the Dome of the Rock.

King Hussein, a direct descendant of the prophet Muhammed who, at the inception of Islam, declared Jerusalem's Mount Moriah to be especially holy for his followers as being the Baitu-l-Mukaddas, the Habitat of Holiness; told me that 'while I have grown accustomed to sorrow, the saddest day of my life was the day of the loss of my grandfather'. Hussein was attracted to the Haram Compound repeatedly in the years that were to follow, not only because of the high degree of holiness of the Aksa and the sanctity of the Dome of the Rock; not only because he is a direct descendant of the prophet Muhammed, but by the magnetic pull of that murder in 1951 which killed his grandfather King Abdullah, whose favourite he was and whom he loved intensely. After the Six Day War of 1967, when Hussein could no longer visit Jerusalem, now all in Israeli hands, he spoke to me of his feelings towards Jerusalem and the Haram Compound, every inch of which is held to be holy to Islam. 'I feel as strongly towards Jerusalem as anyone would feel towards it in the world,' King Hussein said as we sat in his hilltop palace in Amman. Then Hussein added: 'I am sure that it is true that from the point of view of religion, tradition and emotions that Jerusalem is also the heart of Judaism, as it is for the world of Christendom. I believe that the rights of all must be safeguarded in their holy places', before stressing in his talk with me that 'at the same time a solution that is achieved must be one in which Jerusalem does not again have tragedy repeated as in the past. It is the City of Light for the believers in God and it should be that once again.' Even during our fairly brief talk Hussein could not, in talking of the holy places in Jerusalem, but dwell on the murder of his grandfather at, the entrance of the Aksa mosque. Speaking slowly as he recalled that violence which had erupted so many years previously, King Hussein told me that 'for me Jerusalem is important not only because my grandfather was killed there and because my great grandfather, Hussein ibn Ali, the founder of the Arab revolt, is buried there ... but it is extremely important and our rights in Jerusalem are as important to us as nothing else could be.' In his own way King Hussein echoes the hopes for Jerusalem expressed by the prophet Isaiah, desires which are earnestly hoped for by many of the people of Jerusalem today; Jews and Arabs.

Speak ye comfortably to Jerusalem, and cry unto her, that her warfare is accomplished, that her iniquity is pardoned ... O Zion, that bringest good tidings, get thee up into the high mountains; O Jerusalem, that bringest good tidings, lift up thy voice with strength; lift it up, be not afraid ...

It would require a Solomonic judgment, however, to

The cave below the Holy Rock is entered by descending steep steps at the southern side of the Rock. The cave is eight feet high, and its ceiling approximately four or five feet below the upper surface of the rock

A painting of the interior of the Dome of the Rock showing the ornate decoration of gold and multi-coloured glass

reconcile conflicting Jewish and Moslem interests over Mount Moriah, particularly because of the weaving of politics into what should, appropriately, be an exclusive religious matter. It is the expressed aim of the followers of nationalistic extremism among Israelis to make a move in which to demonstrate what they hold to be their sole right to the holy mount, Moriah, and to lay a cornerstone for a new Jewish Temple in the grounds of the Haram. Such a judgment is especially difficult, if not impossible, in our time, not only because of the seething emotions on both sides, but also because the miraculous chain which by Islamic tradition is said to have aided Solomon to deliver true judgment, is no longer there. The Dome of the Chain, only a few paces from the Dome of the Rock is named after this chain which, it is said, was suspended between heaven and earth at this spot during the reign of Solomon.

The following story, which is, in various sources, attributed to Solomon and in others to King David, declares that this chain was possessed of such peculiar virtue that whenever two litigants were unable to decide their quarrel they had but to proceed together to this place, and each endeavour to catch hold of the chain, which would advance to meet the grasp of him who was in the right, and would elude all efforts of the other to catch it. One day, the legend has it, two men appeared before Solomon. One accused the other of owing him money and not returning it. On swearing that he had not received the money back, he put out his hand and, of course, was able to grasp the chain. The fraudulent debtor, having earlier concealed the money in the hollowed staff which he held, handed this to the claimant to 'hold for a moment' and then, swearing that he had returned the money, was also able to grasp the chain firmly. Everybody was perplexed as to the true state of affairs and from that time the chain disappeared, not to be a party to further trickery. It was the Temple built by King Solomon, almost thirty centuries ago, which is held on to as firmly as one would hold on to this chain should it still exist, as being the justification today of both Jews and Moslems to rights on Mount Moriah, and as long as a peacefully agreed compromise is not found, this hilltop will remain a thorn in the flesh of the people of this land and the cause of contention, strife and war. To date neither side are agreed to budge an inch and dark clouds hover over Moriah today, as different clouds hung over the holy mountain when Solomon dedicated and consecrated his House of God in the year 1004 B C. The Bible describes the scene graphically:

There was nothing in the ark save the two tablets of stone, which Moses put there at Horeb, when the Lord made a covenant with the children of Israel, when they came out of the land of Egypt. And it came to pass, when the priests were come out of the holy place, that the cloud filled the house of the Lord. So that the priests could not stand to minister because of the cloud: for the glory of the Lord had filled the house of the Lord. Then spake Solomon, The Lord said that he would dwell in the thick darkness. I have surely built thee an house to dwell in, a settled place for thee to abide in forever ... But will God indeed dwell on the earth behold, the heaven and heaven of heavens cannot contain thee; how much less this house that I have builded? ...

A more fabled account of the consecration of the Temple of Solomon in Islamic lore relates that:

Solomon, when he had built the Consecrated House, and finished it, closed up the gates, and fastened them, lest they should open: nor were they ever opened until he said, after the words of the prayer of his father David, 'Open ye the gates let the gates be opened'. Also, Solomon constituted ten thousand companies of Readers of the children of Israel; five thousand for the day, and five thousand for the night; that there might not be one moment, by night or by day, wherein God was not adored. With respect to opening the gate of the Consecrated House, there was not one of Solomon's attendants who could trust himself to do it. Then came the Spirits of the night to do it; but it was too hard a matter for them. Then he called in the aid of men; but it was too hard for them. Then he asked aid of the genii; but it was too hard for them. Then he sat down in grief, thinking that his Lord had forbidden him to open it: and when he was in this mood, there presented himself before him an old man, leaning upon a staff, and mumbling with his teeth. He was one of the counsellors of David, and he said, O prophet of God! I perceive that you are sad. So he said, I resolved to open this gate; but it was too difficult for me. Then I summoned the assistance of men and of genii, but neither can open it. Then said the old man, Shall I then inform you of the words which thy father David used when he suffered despondency, when also God relieved him of his sorrow. He answered, yes. Then said the old man; 'Say, O God, in thy light will I go the right road; and in thy superabundance will I be satisfied. To thee in the morning, to thee in the evening, will I come. My sins are before thee. Of thee will I ask pardon; and will turn in repentance unto thee, O tenderly merciful! O bounteously gracious!' So, when he said these words, the gate opened.

In dedicating the Temple, King Solomon, according to the biblical account, made it clear that the House of God on Mount Moriah was not to be a place of prayer exclusively for Jews, but indeed for any person who would so wish. The Bible quotes King Solomon in his dedication prayer as beseeching God to hear the prayers at this holy place of those not belonging to Israel, as well.

Moreover concerning a stranger, that is not of thy people Israel, but cometh out of a far country for thy name's sake; (For they shall hear of thy great name, and of thy strong hand, and of thy stretched out arm:) when he shall come and pray towards this house; hear thou in heaven thy dwelling place, and do according to all that the stranger calleth to thee for: that all people of the earth may know thy name, to fear thee, as do thy people Israel; and that they may know that this house, which I have builded, is called by thy name.

It was only after the rise of the Hasmoneans and later during the rule of Herod the Great, with greater power among the Pharisees who more and more leavened religion with gross earthly political ideals, that the Temple was closed to those not of Israel and signs put up warning Gentiles that they would face death should they go beyond a certain point on the Temple Mount. In a book attacking this secularization of religion, the *Assumption of Moses*, which was composed during the lifetime of Jesus of Nazareth, the Hasmonean rulers are termed kings who 'shall call themselves priests of the Most High God: they shall assuredly work iniquity in the holy of holies'. The same author then refers to Herod the Great as 'an insolent king shall succeed them, who will not be of the race of priests, a man bold and shameless, and he shall judge them as they shall deserve ... he shall slay the old and the young, and he shall not spare'. This is attested to by the description of the massacre of the innocents in the New Testament: 'Then Herod, when he saw that he was mocked of the wise men, was exceeding wroth, and sent forth, and slew all the children that were in Bethlehem, and in all the coasts thereof, from two years old and under ... '

Herod received the crown of Jerusalem from Julius Caesar and Mark Antony not only in return for gifts of

vast sums of money, as recorded by the historian
Josephus Flavius, but primarily because he suppressed
the first great Jewish revolt against Rome. This revolt,
headed by Antigonus, was crushed by Herod with great
cruelty. Then the megalomaniac Herod, now king of
Jerusalem, and Judea, wanted, more than anything else, to
be accepted and liked by the people of Israel over
whom he now ruled as a consequence of his cruel
suppression of the Jewish revolt for freedom against
the Romans. A revolt which was ruthlessly crushed by
Herod and which ended with the execution of Antigonus.
Josephus Flavius describes the events with these graphic
and chilling words: 'Now when Antony had received
Antigonus as his captive, he determined to keep him
against his triumph; but when he heard that the nation
grew seditious, and that, out of their hatred to Herod,
they continued to bear goodwill to Antigonus, he resolved
to behead him at Antioch ... Antony seems to have been
the very first man to behead a king, as supposing he could
no other way bend the minds of the Jews so as to receive
Herod, whom he had made king in his stead; for by no
torments could they be forced to call him king, so great a
fondness they had for their former king; so he thought
that this dishonourable death would diminish the value
they had for Antigonus's memory, and at the same time
would diminish the hatred they bare to Herod.'

As the years of Herod's rule continued, the attitude of
the people did not change towards him and this is
illustrated by an incident when ten men conspired to kill
the tyrant but were betrayed by a spy and executed. Says
Josephus of the people's reaction to this: 'Nor was it long
that that spy who had discovered them was seized on by
some of the people, out of the hatred they bore to him;
and was not only slain by them, but pulled to pieces, limb
from limb, and given to the dogs. This execution was

64

A fountain beside the Muthahara Gate, specially anointed for ritual ablutions

El Aksa mosque, with the round pool in the foreground used for ritual ablutions. People sit on the stone steps to wash their feet before entering the mosque

seen by many of the citizens, yet would not one of them discover the doers of it.'

Herod, knowing that the Temple on Mount Moriah served as a shrine to which the Jews were deeply devoted, then felt that, should he build a more magnificent edifice in place of the small Temple which the returnees from the Babylonian exile were able to erect, he would gain that support from the people which he so much desired. In the year 20 B C he set about to begin building such a temple which could not, however, be erected without first pulling down the existing Temple built by Zerubbabel. According to Josephus Herod 'knew that the multitude were not ready nor willing to assist him'. Feelings ran high in Jerusalem and tempers were only barely cooled by the assurance of Herod to the people that 'he would not pull down their temple till all things were gotten ready for building it up entirely' again ... got ready a thousand waggons, that were to bring stones for the building, and chose out ten thousand of the most skilful workmen, and bought a thousand sacerdotal garments for as many of the priests ...' The second Temple was destroyed by Herod and in its stead a truly magnificent building arose, the building of which was made possible only through what many contemporaries called a sell-out to Herod by groups of priests who supported Herod's project in return for political influence. The historian Josephus refers to the destruction of the second Temple in sparse words: 'So Herod took away the old foundations.' An epoch had ended. Describing the building of the third Temple in Jerusalem, that erected by Herod, Josephus specifies the use of tremendously large blocks of hewn stone, the use of which was typical of all the building work of this Idumaean as can be seen today in the remains of the Herodian walls surrounding what was then the Temple Courts; at the Wailing Wall and the south wall west of the

Aksa mosque. These are blocks of stone, some over twenty-five feet long, with each single block of stone weighing a hundred tons and more. No wonder then that this occasioned astonishment when seen for the first time. It was to the Herodian Temple that Jesus came with his disciples and the massive stones were remarked on by the Galileans who had not seen them before, as recorded in the Gospel of Mark: 'And as he went out of the temple, one of his disciples saith unto him, Master, see what manner of stones and what buildings are here!' Describing this Temple, another contemporary, Josephus, wrote that: 'Now the temple was built of stones that were white and strong ... The temple had doors also at the entrance, and lintels over them, of the same height with the temple itself. They were adorned with embroidered veils, with their flowers of purple, and pillars interwoven; and over these, but under the crown-work, was spread out a golden vine, with its branches hanging down from a great height, the largeness and fine workmanship of which was a surprising sight to the spectators ... He also encompassed the entire temple with very large cloisters.' The flat area of the Temple Mount as seen today is to a large extent the result of the work of Herod as he had an entire valley towards the east of Mount Moriah filled in to extend the area of the holy mountain, building a wall around this. The entire area of the Haram today, from north to south, from a line running roughly directly east of the platform of the Dome of the Rock, is this artificial refill of Herod. While the Temple itself was built in just under two years, completed in the year 18 B C, the walls, filling in of this space and the building of the cloisters took eight years. The work involved was stupendous. The Hasmonean tower at the north-western corner of the Temple Mount was improved on and strengthened by Herod and named in honour of Mark Antony. This fortress which controlled the entire Temple Mount, Antonia, had subterranean passages linking it to the Temple Courts, as indeed such passages link this area with the Haram Enclosure today.

It would have been in the cloisters where Jesus heard and disputed with the doctors of the law, as is written: 'they found him in the temple, sitting in the midst of the doctors, both hearing them, and asking them questions. And all that heard him were astonished at his understanding and answers.' Jesus, then, was twelve years old and it would have been among the same cloisters where Jesus was to preach towards the close of His Ministry. Josephus describes the cloisters as having had 'pillars that stood in four rows one over against the other all along, for the fourth row was interwoven into the wall ... and the thickness of each pillar was such, that three men might, with their arms extended, fathom it round, and join their hands again ... These four rows of pillars included three intervals for walking in the middle of this cloister; two of which walks were made parallel to each other, and were contrived after the same manner; the breadth of each of them was thirty feet ... '

In a description of this Temple in the 'Letter of Aristeas' by a contemporary Alexandrian, the atmosphere on the hallowed enclosure is also given: 'The most complete silence reigns so that one might imagine that there was not a single person present, though there are actually seven hundred men engaged in the work, beside the vast number of those who are occupied in bringing up the sacrifices.'

The continuing sacrifices in the Temple did not, however, change the temper of the people towards Herod who failed to gain their approval and when, in March of the year 4 BC, it was known in Jerusalem that Herod was dying, the people poured out, as Josephus puts it, 'to pull down all those works which the king had erected'. They had managed to pull down and break into pieces 'a large golden eagle of great value' which Herod had erected over the 'great gate of the temple' before the soldiers arrived to put an end to this. Forty men were caught and brought before Herod and boldly told him that 'we will undergo death, and all sorts of punishments which thou canst inflict upon us, with pleasure, since we are conscious to ourselves that we shall die, not for any unrighteous actions, but for our love to religion'. Now, as he lay dying, Herod was made fully aware by this act and defiance, that even though he had built a magnificent Temple in Jerusalem, that he was still hated and that most of the people would not accept what he had dedicated to this shrine as being sacred. Herod then gave his last testament which in content and spirit is not different from the political last testament left by another megalomaniac with delusions of grandeur who died in a bunker in Berlin in May, 1945. Drawing again from the description of Josephus, we learn that at the end, Herod declared: 'what principally troubles me is this, that I shall die without being lamented, and without such mourning as men usually expect at a king's death'. With this Herod decreed that 'he shall have a great mourning at his funeral, and such as never had any king before him'. To achieve this, he ordered that 'as soon as they see he hath given up the ghost, they shall place soldiers round the hippodrome, while they do not know that he is dead; and that they shall not declare his death to the multitude till this is done, but that they shall give orders to have those that are in custody shot with their darts; and that this slaughter of them all ... so he took care, when he was departing out of this life, that the whole nation should be put into mourning, and indeed made desolate of their dearest kindred, when he gave order that one out of every family should be slain'.

It is somehow strange that tradition so deeply and indelibly underscores historic truth that the Temple of Herod, destroyed by Titus, is even today referred to as the second Temple, an acceptance that the House of God built by this Herod was simply a continuation of that built by Zerubbabel. When, today, the vast works of Herod are uncovered in archaeological excavations at the western and southern walls of the Temple Mount, these are referred to as being sacred relics of the second Temple; Herod, twenty centuries after his death, is receiving that acclamation and acceptance which the people of Jerusalem and Judea refused to give him in his lifetime. While there is some irony in this, it is nevertheless also true that the significance of the Temple, even that of Herod, and the sacred attributes of Mount Moriah, are for the Jews of far greater import than the character and motives of Herod who created the buildings and walls, some of which remain to this day. It is one of the Herodian built walls enclosing the Temple Mount, the western wall, also known as the Wailing Wall, which has attracted Jews as a place of prayer and supplication, holding this to be a tangible link with the Temple which stood on Mount Moriah so many long centuries ago.

The Temple was, indeed, generally accepted as such by the people after the death of Herod. Its destruction by Titus, seventy-four years after the death of Herod, when another generation was living in Jerusalem, was felt as the most heart-rending catastrophe which could have befallen the people of Israel. The people, indeed, tried to defend the Temple from destruction only a few months after Herod's death when the Roman Varus came to Jerusalem to crush a revolt. Part of the cloisters were burnt at this time and many perished in the flames after which, Josephus records, Varus had two thousand men crucified

(*Above*) *A cedar wood decoration of El Aksa, dating back to the original 7th-century building*

(*Above right*) *Moslem overflow at prayer. While the Aksa mosque can hold five thousand people, tens of thousands more devout Moslems have to be content to pray in the spacious courts between the Aksa and the Dome of the Rock*

(*Right*) *The interior of the Aksa mosque. It was damaged by fire in 1969, the roof below the silver dome and the south-eastern section of the mosque being devoured*

in Jerusalem, an event also referred to in another contemporary document, the *Assumption of Moses*, whose author wrote that: 'a powerful king of the west shall come, who shall conquer them: and he shall take them captive, and burn part of their temple with fire, and shall crucify some'.

The stage was set for the end as the Jews of Israel refused to knuckle under the Roman yoke, refused to worship Caesar as a deity and, having removed the last vestiges of paganism introduced into Jerusalem by Herod, and without being under fear of a tyrannical and cruel ruler, returned to their true Temple worship. Not that this genuine religious fevour of the people was not exploited by those leaders who used the religious emotions of the people for their own political ends. It was these leaders who came under such scathing attack by those who strove for true faith and not for the politization of religion. Thus the attacks on the Pharisees by Jesus and even stronger attacks on the Pharisee leaders as recently found in the documents of the Community of the Dead Sea Scrolls. So, also, attacks on Sadducees, by the author of the *Assumption of Moses*, who wrote that: 'these destructive and impious men shall rule, saying that they are just ... treacherous men, self-pleasers, dissemblers in all their own affairs and lovers of banquets at every hour of the day, gluttons ... '

The stage was set for the end in the second great Jewish revolt against Rome which began in the year A D 66, the first having been that suppressed by Herod a century earlier. In the year A D 70 Titus besieged Jerusalem and burnt the Temple. The people of Israel went into exile and were dispersed over the face of the world. After the destruction of Solomon's Temple, it was less than half a century after the start was made to rebuild the Temple and re-establish Jewish independence in the

Holy Land. The destruction of Jerusalem and the Temple by the Romans was a far greater calamity, however. It was nineteen centuries before an independent Israel could arise once more. Josephus Flavius, who was present in Jerusalem when the city was captured and the Temple burnt down, described this cataclysmic event in these words: ' ... these Romans put the Jews to flight, and proceeded as far as the holy house itself. At which time one of the soldiers, without staying for any orders, and without any concern or dread upon him at so great an undertaking, and being hurried on by a certain divine fury, snatched somewhat out of the materials that were on fire, and being lifted up by another soldier, he set fire to a golden window, through which there was a passage to the rooms that were round about the holy house, on the north side of it. As the flames went upward, the Jews made a great clamour, such as so mighty an affliction required, and ran together to prevent it; and now they spared not their lives any longer, nor suffered anything to restrain their force, since that holy house was perishing ... thus it was the holy house burnt down ... Nor can one imagine any thing either greater or more terrible than this noise; for there was at once a shout of the Roman Legions, who were marching all together, and a sad clamour of the seditious, who were now surrounded with fire and sword ... the people under a great consternation, made sad moans at the calamity they were under ... Yet was the misery itself more terrible than this disorder; for one would have thought that the hill itself, on which the temple stood, was seething hot, as full of fire on every part of it ... '

For the Jews this was, until they regained their freedom in the land of Israel in the twentieth century, the end of the world. As a first century A D writer put it: 'The horns of the sun shall be broken and shall be turned into darkness, and the moon shall not give her light and be turned into blood.'

Et cornua solis confringentur et in tenebras convertet se;
Et luna non dabit lumen et tota convertet se in sanguinem.

Mount Moriah, and the sacred shrines later built on it, were not spared further calamities and catastrophes in the centuries which were to follow, but nothing to the extent and import of that autumn day in the year A D 70. A series of earthquakes caused damage, mainly to the Aksa mosque. In A D 746 an earthquake badly damaged the Aksa mosque which was repaired by the Abbaside Caliphs, al-Mansur and al-Mahdi. Both the eastern and western portions of the mosque collapsed as a result of damage by this earthquake. It is written that the Caliph Abu Ja'far al Mansur, not having sufficient funds for the repair work, ordered that the plates of gold and silver which overlaid the doors should be stripped off. The Aksa mosque had hardly been rebuilt when 'it fell down again' as a result of another earthquake in A D 755 and was only rebuilt much later by the Caliph Omar ibn 'Abd al Aziz al Mahdi. There was another great earthquake felt in Jerusalem in A D 846 and a story is told that during a night, that year, the guards of the Dome of the Rock 'were suddenly astonished to find the dome itself replaced, so that they could see the stars and feel the rain splashing upon their faces. They then heard a low voice saying gently, "Put it straight again", and gradually it settled down into its ordinary state.' Yet another earthquake shook Mount Moriah less than two centuries later and this time, in the year A D 1016, the great cupola of the Dome of the Rock collapsed although there was not any severe damage to the rest of the building. The dome over the sacred rock was repaired six years later but in A D 1033 another earthquake shook Jerusalem. This caused great damage to the Aksa mosque. An Arab historian, al-Yahya, relates that the earthquake of 1033 was thought to have been punishment for the use by adh Dhahir, of stones from demolished churches, to rebuild the walls of Jerusalem. Says al-Yahya: 'the work was interrupted by a devastating earthquake' and that adh Dhahir immediately began reconstructing the Aksa mosque, work which was completed by his successor al-Mustansir. Nine centuries without serious earthquakes were to follow until the Holy Land was rocked by a catastrophic quake in 1927 which caused high casualties in Jerusalem, Safed and Tiberias as well as severe damage in these three towns. Again the Aksa mosque was damaged and as in most previous cases, nothing serious happened to the Dome of the Rock so close to it. The whole of the nave was rebuilt and work continued until 1943. It was at this time that the present pillars of white Italian marble were introduced.

Then came the disastrous fire in the Aksa mosque on Thursday, 21st August, 1969, and, again, it was given to me to be a spectator of history; to stand inside the Aksa while it burnt and to witness the emotions of Moslems there while flames swept through their holy place, part of the Baitu-l-Mukaddas, the Habitat of Holiness. I had returned to Jerusalem only shortly before from a visit to Egypt where, among other things, I examined the slender remains still visible of the Jewish Temple at Leontopolis which functioned, with the legitimate High Priests of the family of Zadok, from 154 BC until two or three years after the burning by Titus of the Jerusalem Temple in AD 70, when I was to witness this latest fire of a holy place on this same Mount Moriah. The anguish was something terrible to behold. In the faces of men and women standing that morning beside and inside the burning Aksa one could see the pain and suffering welling up from

75

the soul as they watched the flames devour parts of their mosque standing on a spot where, traditionally, the prophet Muhammed himself had prayed. There were the sounds, a chant which sounded like a roar, of the words 'Allah Akbar' – Allah is Great – from the throats of hundreds who tried to quench the fire with buckets, which they filled from a fire engine which raced into the nave of the mosque while dozens of Arab youths clung to it shouting 'Allah Akbar'. Outside other fire engines, Israeli and Arab, fought the blaze which was finally put out. The roof below the silver dome and the roof over the south-eastern section of the mosque had been devoured by the fire. One of the finest pieces of art in the world, the mimbar, or pulpit, was a pile of smoking ashes upon which burnt-out beams of wood collapsed from time to time. Made by an artist in Aleppo in AD 1168 and with an inscription in the name of the Sultan Nur-ed-Din who had resolved to conquer Jerusalem from the Crusaders, the pulpit was perhaps the most exquisite piece of carved woodwork in the world. Immediately after taking Jerusalem, Saladin had sent to Aleppo to bring this pulpit to be placed in the Jami' al-Aksa, where it stood and was admired by countless visitors during the centuries which followed, until it was destroyed in the fire set, under it, by the Australian psychopath, Michael Rohan.

That same afternoon a high ranking delegation of Israeli leaders led by the Prime Minister, Mrs Golda Meir, went to the Aksa mosque, part of which was gutted, and here Mrs Meir expressed her sorrow and shock at the calamity which had so suddenly come to strike at the holy Aksa. Mrs Meir, who was received by Sheikh al Ansari beside the Aksa, spoke with sincerity which was obvious to those who, like myself, heard not only her words but their tone and who saw her reactions in looking at the damage

(*Right*) *A small cupola on the Temple Mount esplanade*

(*Below*) *The platform on which the Dome of the Rock stands*

(*Bottom left*) *The white-sculptured marble pulpit on the southern edge of the platform of the Dome of the Rock*

(*Bottom right*) *A close-up etching of a cupola in the enclosure of the Haram-as-Sherif*

caused by the fire. I noted the same attitude and reaction among the other Israeli leaders who had joined the Prime Minister beside and in the Aksa that grim afternoon. There was the Deputy Premier, Mr Yigal Allon; the Minister of Police, Mr Eliyahu Sasson, and the Minister of Defence, General Moshe Dayan. Dayan told the leader of the Moslem Wakf, Hassan Tahboub, that the Israeli Government would do everything possible to facilitate the repair of the Aksa and that he would give permission to any expert from other Arab countries who may be needed, to enter Israel in order to facilitate this repair work.

Feelings were running high in Jerusalem and beyond. While many Arabs openly accused the Jews of having burnt the Aksa, emotions were quickly fanned and ugly riots erupted in the Old City of Jerusalem the next day. Michael Rohan was arrested and made a full confession and at noon on this Friday the police informed the Government of this. This circumstance makes all the more inexplicable a statement made the Friday evening by an Israeli Cabinet Minister, Mr Israel Galili. Broadcast at six-thirty on Friday evening, long after the Cabinet – and presumably also Mr Galili – had been informed by the police of how the fire had started and the identity of the person who had started it, he accused the Arabs themselves of possibly having set fire to their own holy place to use this as a provocation with which to attack Israel. This statement by Mr Galili would have gone unnoticed, had it not been for the fact that the Israeli Government Press Office distributed an English translation of the Minister's strange statement to foreign correspondents, a bare hour before the Israeli police called a press conference to announce the arrest of Michael Rohan for setting fire to the Aksa mosque. It was the publication of this document by the Press Office

which reflects not only the intolerance which mars inter-
racial and inter-religious life in Jerusalem today, but
which acted as a counter-weight to the genuine expres-
sions of sorrow and sympathy for the Moslems expressed
the previous afternoon beside the Aksa by Mrs Meir, the
Prime Minister, and the other three Cabinet Ministers
who had gone with her to so express the general Israeli
feelings of sadness at the burning of the mosque. Appar-
ently thinking that it would be useful to get in a few
quick political licks before the truth was to be revealed by
the Israeli police that Friday evening, the head of the
Government Press Office, a gentleman by the name of
Landor, put out the communique with a time embargo of
six-thirty on that same Friday evening in which the vile
calumny that Arabs had set fire to their own shrine was
made available to the world press; at a time when all the
facts were already well known by the authorities at all
levels, as was later revealed at the Commission of Inquiry
which investigated the cause of the fire. The Government
Press Office communique quotes Minister Galili as saying
that 'the Arabs are misusing the disaster which happened
in the al Aksa mosque, irrespective whether it was caused
by a short circuit or was a case of provocation ... I am not
saying that this was indeed a case of provocation, but
neither can I exclude such a possibility ... if you ask me as
a statesman who is fully aware of the attitudes of the Arab
rulers, the Fatach people and other elements – if it is
conceivable that in this Arab world such an act of provocation could have been carried out, my answer is
definitely in the affirmative.'

This statement was distributed by the Press Office after
the Minister of Police had already officially informed the
Moslem leaders of Jerusalem of the arrest of Rohan. The
conflict of interest over Mount Moriah is difficult and
complicated and if peaceful solutions are to be found

which would satisfy the religious interests there of both Jews and Moslems, then cooler counsels will have to prevail. The goodwill engendered by the Prime Minister in this case was quickly negated by the distribution of this document.

It was not only tragedy and sorrow which rested on Mount Moriah during the ages in which it was held sacred and there were occasions of joy here, too. The historians Besant and Palmer give this description of the scene in the Dome of the Rock after it was completed and thrown open to worship.

'No expense or trouble was spared to make it as attractive as possible to the worshippers. Every morning a number of attendants were employed in pounding saffron, and in making perfumed water with which to sprinkle the building, as well as in preparing and burning incense. Servants were also sent into the Hamman Suleiman (Solomon's bath). Then they used to go into the store-room where the *khaluk* (an aromatic plant) was kept, and changing their clothes for fresh ones of costly stuffs, and putting jewelled girdles round their waists, and taking the *khaluk* in their hands, they proceeded to dab it all over the Sakhrah as far as they could reach; and when they could not reach with their hands they washed their feet and stepped upon the Sakhrah itself until they had dabbed it all over, and emptied the pots of *khaluk*. Then they brought censers of gold and silver filled with *ud* (perfumed aloes wood) and other costly kinds of incense, with which they perfumed the entire place, first letting down the curtains round all the pillars, and walking round them until the incense filled the place between them and the dome, and then fastening them up again so that the incense escaped and filled the entire building, even penetrating into the neighbouring bazaar, so that anyone who passed that way could smell it. After this proclamation was made in the public market; "The Sakhrah is now open for public worship", and people would run in such crowds to pray there, that two *reka'as* – prostrations – was as much as most men could accomplish, and it was only a very few who could succeed in performing four.

'So strongly was the building perfumed with the incense, that one who had been into it could at once be detected by the odour, and people used to say as they sniffed it, "Aha, So and So has been in the Sakhrah". So great, too, was the throng, that people could not perform their ablutions in the orthodox manner, but were obliged to content themselves with washing the soles of their feet with water, wiping them with green sprigs of myrtle, and drying them with their pocket-handkerchiefs.'

The attitudes so expressed by Moslems in the seventh century, have persisted to the present and, at times, while the Aksa mosque can hold five thousand people, tens of thousands more devout Moslems have to be content to pray in the spacious courts between the Aksa and the Dome of the Rock. The accusation that Arabs are capable of burning down their own, so hallowed shrine as the Aksa as to be found in the communique distributed by the Israeli Government Press Office, can only be seen as an attempt at exacerbating relations between Jew and Arab in Jerusalem by using cheap propaganda in an attempt at denigrating the Arabs, particularly in the timing of this communique, a bare hour before the official announcement to the world that the fire in the Aksa mosque had indeed been deliberately lit by Michael Denis Rohan. That the dissemination of hate propaganda was completely against the policy of the Israeli Government and the sentiments of just men, is something which nevertheless did not deter that individual responsible from distributing so shocking a document.

The Noble Sanctuary of today, the Haram as-Sherif, has a number of gates in the walls leading to it. Three of these on the southern wall are closed while the Golden Gate set in the eastern wall is also sealed. This Golden Gate is the double gateway called the gates of Mercy and Redemption, by both Jews and Moslems. There are three gates in the northern wall of the Haram and eight gateways set in the western wall, the central of which is the Gate of the Chain which comprises two domed vaults. There is the Hittah Gate, meaning the gate of Remission, based on the instructions in the Koran to 'enter the gate with adoration and say "Remission" .' Particularly attractive is the Cotton-merchants Gate. There is a gate named Reconciliation, where by tradition God was reconciled with David after his sin of taking Bathsheba while she was still married to another.

There is the Moor Gate beside the Wailing Wall which, since 1967, has become a cause of friction between Israelis and Moslems. The key to this gate was taken by the Israeli Army and free entry was, and is, permitted to the Haram Compound through it to the chagrin of the Moslem Council who at one stage tried to collect the normal entry price at this gate, except to have this prevented by the authorities. After the Aksa fire all gates, including the Moor Gate, were closed to visitors, but then politics again came into play. Elections were due in Israel and extremist nationalistic groups began making much of the issue that the Government of Israel, could it be imagined, was actually preventing Jews from entering their own most sacred place – Mount Moriah. The result was that, despite Moslem protests, the Moor Gate was again swung open by government order for free entry of visitors to the Haram Compound. Shortly afterwards the Moslem authorities also re-opened another entry gate to the enclosure. Official Israeli pronouncements declared

A muezzin calls the Faithful to prayer five times a day

North-west quarter of Temple Mount with a minaret in the background. This most splendid of the four minarets on Temple Mount was built in 1329

that the Moslems would be able to retain absolute and complete control of their mosques and shrines of the Temple Mount but that the grounds themselves would be under government control. This compromise satisfied neither of the contending factions, however, and pressures are continuing to build up, on the one hand to reinstate Moslem control over entry of all visitors to the Haram as-Sherif, and on the other hand to permit Jews to openly and regularly pray within the walled enclosure as a first step not only to demonstrate what the protagonists call 'Israel's sovereignity' over Mount Moriah, but as a move to rebuild the Temple.

Time passed and tempers cooled so that today there is peaceful co-existence. All the gates are kept open by the Moslem authorities and the Israeli police prevent Jews from demonstratively praying in the Haram Compound.

In AD 1229 Frederick II of Hohenstaufen, Emperor of Germany and thrice excommunicated by the Pope, became king of Jerusalem after the city was surrendered without a sword's blow by the Sultan Malek al-Kamil. The terms of the treaty, signed on the 18th February that year, were that while Jerusalem and Bethlehem would form part of the Christian kingdom, the Temple Mount with the Dome of the Rock and the Aksa mosque would remain in Moslem hands, and Moslems were to be allowed the right of entry and freedom of worship. This treaty was bitterly condemned by both Moslems and Christians as politics came into play. Horrified Moslems declared a state of mourning 'for the betrayal by al-Kamil' and, as Steven Runciman puts it in his *History of the Crusades*: 'Even al-Kamil's own imams abused him to his face; and his lame reply that he had only ceded ruined houses and churches, while the Moslem shrines were intact and saved for the Faith, was little consolation

The more intransigent (of the Christians) lamented that

Jerusalem had not been won back by the sword, and were disgusted that the infidel should retain their shrines.'

What happened after Frederick entered Jerusalem on Saturday, the 17th March, 1229, is described by Runciman: 'Frederick's own companions were embarrassed by his excommunication ... next morning, Sunday the 18th, Frederick went to attend Mass in the Church of the Holy Sepulchre. Not a priest was there ... it was with relief that Frederick turned aside from his work to visit the Moslem shrines. The Sultan had tactfully ordered the Muezzin at al-Aksa not to make the call to prayer while the Christian sovereign was in the city. But Frederick protested. The Moslems must not change their customs because of him. Besides, he said, he had come to Jerusalem in order to hear the Muezzin's call through the night. As he entered the holy area of the Haram as-Sherif he noticed a Christian cleric following behind. He at once himself rudely ejected him, and gave orders that any Christian priest that crossed the threshold without permission from the Moslems should be put to death.'

Today one can obtain permission, however, to enter the Haram Area which is closed to visitors only during the hours of prayer and during the month of Ramadan. There are many interesting things to see apart from the Dome of the Rock and the Aksa mosque. There are four minarets in the Haram. The one at the south-western corner dates from the year 1278 and the minaret rising above the Gate of the Chain from AD 1329. The most beautiful of the four, that at the north-western corner was also built in 1329. It stands, partly, on the site of the fortress of Antonia built by the Hasmoneans and strengthened by Herod the Great. This minaret is linked to the Haram Courts by a staircase as Antonia was twenty centuries ago. It was on these stairs that Paul stood from where to address the people in his celebrated defence after his arrest: 'Men, brethren and fathers, hear ye my defence which I make now unto you ...' While the upper part of the fourth Haram minaret, in the north-eastern corner is modern, its base dates back to A D 1367.

There is a small dome near the Dome of the Rock and to its west, called the Cubbet el M'iraj (Dome of the Ascent), which marks the spot from which Muhammed is supposed to have started his 'heavenly journey'. The present dome was built in the year A D 697. The white sculptured marble pulpit nearby, at the southern edge of the platform of the Dome of the Rock, is said to have been built on the spot where Muhammed stood in contemplation and prayer before his 'ascent to heaven', and is thus called the 'Macam an-Nebi' – the Place of the Prophet.

At the end of the Haram Compound, on the eastern side, is a place called the 'Market of Knowledge' – the Suk el Ma'rifah. Legends woven about this place say that it is said to be beside the place where King David prayed. It is written 'that when in ancient times any Jewish resident of Jerusalem had committed a sin, he would write up the facts on the door of his house and then promptly proceed to the Market of Knowledge to pray for forgiveness. If he obtained his request, tradition had it, he found the written confession obliterated from his door on his return home. However, if the writing was still there, the unfortunate sinner 'was rigorously cut off from all communication with his fellow men until the miraculous signature of pardon was accorded him'.

There is a well just to the west of the Aksa mosque, an extraordinary well which gives a direct link to Paradise itself. Called the 'Bir el Warakah' – the Well of the Leaf, because of the tradition which is said to prove this extraordinary fact, it is held in great reverence to this day. It is written:

The following tale is told: Muhammed had said that a divine revelation had asserted as follows, 'Truly, there shall be a man of your people who shall assuredly enter into Paradise, although he be walking upon his two feet, and be still alive'. Now, says an old worthy, I was standing before the congregation in the Holy Abode, who were engaged in prayer, with the people of Omar ibn al-Khatab, when there arrived a certain Taminite, named Sharik ibn Habash. He was drawing water for his comrades, when his bucket, or pitcher, fell into the well. Descending to bring it up, he found a gate in the well, opening to the Angel-land by which he walked into the said land, and took some leaves of the trees thereof. This took place after the summons to prayer. He then returned to the well and climbed up. This story being told to the governor of the Baitu-l-Mukaddas, he sent for the man, and with several others went down himself, into the well; but they found no gate, nor any angels or genii. This being communicated to Omar, he replied that this was a verification of Muhammed's assertion. He also desired them to remark the leaves. If they dried up and changed, they were not the leaves of Paradise, which wither not. It is said that they neither dried up nor changed. Some say that the man was in the mountain of the Holy Abode, and that, having descended into the well, to bring up his bucket, a personage appeared unto him, and said, Come along with me. So, taking him by the hand, he brought him into Paradise, whence Sharik having plucked the leaves, he replaced him on the same spot where he had stood before ... the leaves were found to be of surpassing fragrance and sweetness.

There are two other supposed entrances to Paradise in the Haram as-Sherif; one under the Aksa mosque and the other below the Sakhrah, that rock under the Dome of the Rock which by tradition is one of the rocks of Paradise itself, 'standing on a palm-tree, beneath which flows one of the rivers of Paradise'. It is written that 'beneath the shade of this tree Asia, the wife of Pharaoh, the most beautiful woman in the world and Miriam the sister of Moses shall stand on the Day of Resurrection, to give drink to true believers'. There is a large rock in the substructures of the Aksa mosque which is believed to block up one entrance to the netherworld. This rock, six feet high, over four feet long and almost four feet wide, lies about midway among the eastern arcades in the extensive vaults under the Aksa. It is behind this rock, where, by tradition, King Solomon tortured a demon. The story is told of those who believed that this tale was simply invented to frighten away people in order to protect a supposed treasure hidden behind the rock. They tried to remove the rock with pickaxes in order to get at this treasure. The very first blow, however, led the devil to cry out 'let me alone' and the treasure-seekers fled. Since then there has been no individual brave enough to attempt to move this rock to the passage beyond it.

The third entrance to Paradise, today covered by a fine piece of green marble, some fifteen inches square, is in the Dome of the Rock. Called the 'Bir Arruah' – the Well of Souls – it is fastened down with a number of gilt nails. This is said to be the door to Paradise and a number of holes in the marble indicate that, in former times, it was held down with more nails than the number which presently seals off what is below it. It is written that these nails had been pulled out by the devil when he wanted to enter Paradise but this scheme was foiled as the devil could not extract all the nails. It is generally believed that this entrance to Paradise was open until about the end of the eighteenth century A D and that while so open, the place was frequented by those 'who were desirous of holding converse with the souls of the departed confined below'. However, after 'a certain widow, who was more

*A Fountain just outside Temple Mount used for
ritual ablutions outside the Gate of the Chain*

than ordinarily curious and communicative, carried such intelligence from the living to the dead, and from the dead to the living, as to disturb the peace of many families in the city, and caused such commotions below, that the noise getting too outrageous, the well had to be closed to prevent further mischief-making'. Another common explanation for the removal of the nails in this marble slab over the Well of Souls, is that it was formerly held down by eighteen nails and is held to be a kind of chronological table. A nail was withdrawn for each grand epoch in history, 'and when the last nail takes flight, the consummation of all things will occur'.

From the outside, the Dome of the Rock with its luxuriant covering of porcelain tiles of the richest colours, appears as if the building has no windows at all. It is only from the inside, in the dim suffused light that one notes that the circular body of the building is pierced with sixteen windows of such rich stained glass to find its equal in splendour only in the cathedral of Chartres. In the lower section of the Dome of the Rock there are seven stained glass windows set in each of its eight sides, all absolutely magnificent and superbly exquisite in their beauty. Looking up, the gold motif of the ceiling is something else of superlative beauty so that it is no exaggeration at all to designate the Dome of the Rock in Jerusalem as one of the most beautiful and aesthetic buildings in the world – if not the most beautiful of all buildings which man has built.

There are numerous sights to be seen in the Haram Enclosure, many things with rich associations to the history of Jerusalem. The sixth-century historian, Procopius of Caesarea, wrote that the Emperor Justinian had built a church in Jerusalem. It is generally accepted that the Aksa mosque, when it was built a century and a half later, incorporated in its structure parts of this church of Justinian. In the vaults under the Aksa, used by the Crusader Knights to stable their horses, one can still see the iron rings to which they tethered them. One can also see a pillar which had been originally used in the building of the temple to Jupiter in the second century and dedicated to Hadrian, in these subterranean vaults. When this pillar was re-used it was placed upside down and the inscription is still to be read – upside down. It is written that after Justinian built his church, it was so magnificent, that 'in the delight of his heart, the Emperor exclaimed, "I have surpassed thee, O Solomon".' Walking in the dim light in the underground chambers below the Aksa one finds, at the south-western corner, a place called the 'Sidna Isa' – the Cradle of Jesus. It is said that this subterranean oratory is the place where Mary, the mother of Jesus, performed her devotions.

There is the Wailing Wall. While the first record that the Jews made it a custom to pray at the Wailing Wall is that made by the twelfth-century A D traveller, Benjamin of Tudela, an inscription of verses from Isaiah carved into the living rock in the fourth century uncovered in recent archaeological excavations, shows that the tradition is an old, time-honoured one. In earlier times it was a practice among the Jews to drive iron nails between the crevices between the massive blocks of rock of the Wailing Wall, in order to leave 'a nail in his holy place' as written in the Book of Ezra: 'And now for a little space grace hath been shewed from the Lord our God, to leave us a remnant to escape, and give us a nail in his holy place, that our God may lighten our eyes, and give us a little reviving in our bondage.'

Since it is not certain that Salem, where the Patriarch Abraham met the king Melchizedek, was indeed a city where Jerusalem stands today we must accept that the first record of a city called today Jerusalem, is to be found in the Tell-el-Amarna tablets. These letters were sent to the Egyptian Pharaoh's Amenhotep III and his son, Amenhotep IV by their consuls and allies in Syria and Palestine. That was some three thousand five hundred years ago. Ever since then the records of history tell of a special place which Jerusalem has held in the hearts and minds of sons of men.

The Koran says: 'Proclaim unto the people a solemn pilgrimage; let them come unto thee on foot, and on every lean camel, arriving from every distant road; that they be witnesses of the advantages which accrue from visiting this holy place.' When this was written, the prophet Muhammed had Jerusalem in mind.

The prophet Isaiah wrote: 'How beautiful upon the mountains are the feet of him that bringeth good tidings, that publisheth peace; that bringeth good tidings of good, that publisheth salvation; that sayeth unto Zion, Thy God reigneth! Thy watchman shall lift up the voice; with the voice together shall they sing: for they shall see eye to eye, when the Lord shall bring again Zion. Break forth into joy, sing together, ye waste places of Jerusalem for the Lord hath comforted his people, he hath redeemed Jerusalem.'

Jews praying at the Western Wall (or Wailing Wall). An inscription of verses from Isaiah carved in the 4th century and uncovered in recent excavations indicates that the tradition of praying at the Wall is an old and time-honoured one (Photograph by David Rubinger)

These are the wars fought in and for JERUSALEM

BC

1428 Razed by the Israelites

1049 Captured by King David

970 Plundered by Shishak

844 Plundered by the Philistines

808 Taken by King Jehoash of the Northern Israel Kingdom

710 Besieged by Sennacherib

610 Taken by Pharaoh Necho

598 Plundered by Nebuchadnezzar

586 Taken by the Chaldeans

320 Captured by Ptolemy Soter

314 Taken by Antiochus the Great

301 Taken by Ptolemy Epiphanes

170 Captured by Antiochus Epiphanes

166 Captured by Judas Maccabaeus

164 Besieged by Antiochus Eupator

126 Besieged by Antiochus Soter

65 Besieged by Aretas

63 Captured by Pompey

40 Captured by the Parthians

38 Taken by Herod the Great

AD

70 Razed by Titus

135 Sacked by Hadrian

614 Taken by the Persians

629 Captured by Heraclius

94

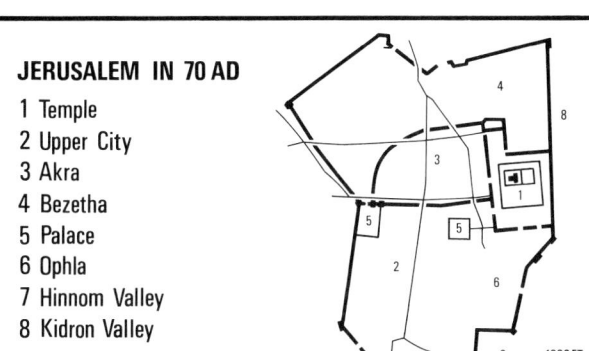

JERUSALEM IN 70 AD

1 Temple
2 Upper City
3 Akra
4 Bezetha
5 Palace
6 Ophla
7 Hinnom Valley
8 Kidron Valley

637 Captured by the Saracens under Omar ibn al-Khatab

1076 Atsiz takes Jerusalem from the Caliph al-Mostanther Billah

1095 al-Afdhal ibn Bedr captures the city for Egypt after 40-day siege

1099 The Crusaders, under Godfrey de Bouillon, capture Jerusalem

1187 Captured by Salah-ed-Din

1244 Sacked by the Mongol Hordes

1247 Captured by the Carizmians

1517 Selim 1 takes the city bringing it into the Ottoman Empire

1822 Taken by Ibrahim Pasha of Egypt

1917 Captured by General Allenby of Britain

1948 War between the newly established Israel against Jordan and Egypt in Jerusalem after which part of the city remains under Israeli rule and part under Jordan

1967 The Old City of Jerusalem falls to Israeli arms

95

Index